James A. Erskine
Michiel R. Leenders
Louise A. Mauffette-Leenders

teaching with cases

third edition

Richard Ivey School of Business
The University of Western Ontario

IVEY

Teaching with Cases
THIRD EDITION

ISBN   0-7714-2419-1

This book may be ordered from:

Ivey Publishing
Richard Ivey School of Business
The University of Western Ontario
London, Ontario, Canada, N6A 3K7

Phone: (+1) 519-661-3208
Fax: (+1) 519-661-3882
E-mail: cases@ivey.uwo.ca
Websites: http://www.ivey.uwo.ca/cases
          http://www.ivey.uwo.ca/workshops

about the authors

James A. Erskine teaches Operations Management at the Richard Ivey School of Business. He has Engineering and MBA degrees from The University of Western Ontario and a doctorate from Indiana University. Over the past 35 years Jim has conducted case method workshops and management development programs for thousands of participants in more than 30 countries. In 1986, Jim received the 3-M teaching fellow award recognizing him as one of Canada's best university professors. In 2000, he received the Edward G. Pleva teaching excellence award, the highest teaching honor at The University of Western Ontario. In 2001, he received the Bank of Nova Scotia, UWO Alumni Association and Students' Council award of excellence in undergraduate teaching.

Michiel R. Leenders is the Purchasing Management Association of Canada Professor Emeritus at the Richard Ivey School of Business. He received a degree in Mining Engineering from the University of Alberta, an M.B.A. from The University of Western Ontario and his doctorate from the Harvard Business School. He is a former director of the School's Ph.D. program and has taught and consulted extensively both in Canada and internationally. Mike's texts have been translated into eight different languages. He has authored and co-authored nine books in the supply management field. In 1997, Mike received the Leaders in Management Education Award sponsored by the Financial Post and Bell Canada.

Louise A. Mauffette-Leenders holds a BA from Collège Jean-de-Brébeuf, a BBA and MBA from l'École des Hautes Études Commerciales of Montréal, Québec. As case writer and research associate at the Richard Ivey School of Business at The University of Western Ontario, she wrote dozens of cases in all areas of management, including the non-profit sector. Since 1987, Louise has worked in the social services as well as non-government organizations with development programs in India and Peru. She has written and taught cases in various training programs for social services providers.

acknowledgements

The ideas contained in this text have been nurtured and shaped by the thousands of aspiring and experienced teachers throughout the world who have participated in our case method workshops for more than 35 years. They provide proof that teaching with cases is indeed universal.

We are grateful to our colleagues at the Ivey Business School for their input, help and encouragement. They continue to raise the bar for effective case teaching.

We have been privileged with the opportunity to listen to and learn from a steady stream of highly motivated and competent students in our classes and courses. Their genuine interest and high expectations in augmenting their skills and abilities through case discussion has given us a living laboratory to test the ideas in this book.

The Harvard Business School pioneered the case method for use in management education. We are most appreciative of our Harvard colleagues who have freely shared their insights, experience and advice for many many years.

We value highly the people at the European Case Clearing House for their work in disseminating cases and case literature and for providing opportunities for others to learn. They make it easier for teachers to access materials and augment their skills.

Finally, we are very thankful for the work of Elaine Carson assisted by Sharon Rochard. They prepared the several iterations of the text copy with great skill and patience. We are indebted to their proficiency and continuous support.

preface

We are delighted to offer this third edition of *Teaching with Cases*. Fully integrated with *Learning with Cases*, it forms a valuable two-volume set for anyone interested in the case teaching/learning process.

Our first and second editions of *Teaching with Cases* were largely descriptive, based on the literature and personal interviews with over 100 case teachers. This new version while still building on the strengths of the first two editions, has been extensively revised based on our experiences in teaching regular classes and feedback from case method workshops around the world. We have expanded significantly on managing the participative process with special emphasis on questioning and responding. The proven concept of the Case Teaching Plan joins our other concepts of the Case Difficulty Cube, The Three Stage Learning Process and the Case Preparation Chart to improve the efficiency and effectiveness of case teaching.

Experienced case instructors can sharpen their teaching skills by benchmarking their own performance against the ideas presented in this text, while new case teachers can get started faster and more effectively. Both veterans and newcomers alike can counsel students better using the cause and effect analysis presented in the feedback and counselling chapter. Anyone seriously interested in case teaching can use the tips, tactics and techniques spread throughout this book to experience more fully the joy of teaching with cases.

contents

introduction

The excitement of effective learning and teaching with cases provides a unique and extremely satisfying experience to the case teacher and to his or her students. We are convinced that every teacher using cases can improve his or her performance and will find this text helpful.

Almost a century ago the Harvard Business School chose the case method as an effective way of teaching business administration. Today the use of cases is no longer the preserve of a few selected schools of business. Cases are now taught around the world in a wide variety of disciplines. Participatory and collaborative learning, using descriptions of decisions faced in real life by real managers, has proven to be an exciting alternative to more traditional forms of education. Teaching with cases, however, presents unique challenges to instructors. That is why this book was written.

This book is part of the authors' trilogy covering case writing, case learning and case teaching. The previous editions of *Teaching with Cases* were based largely on the literature available and interviews with over a hundred case teachers from around the world. This third edition builds on this heritage and our experience of instructing over eight thousand teachers in case teaching workshops over the past thirty-five years. The authors themselves count over a hundred years of case learning and teaching experience. They have class-tested and proven the effectiveness of all the key ideas advanced in this text.

Cases give students and instructors the same information from which decisions are to be made. From this starting point, each will obviously play a distinctly different role in the process of learning. Exhibit 1-1 summarizes the teacher and student roles in a regular case class.

Exhibit 1-1
THE TEACHER AND STUDENT ROLES
IN A REGULAR CASE CLASS

When	Professor	Student or Participant
Before Class	Assigns a case and, often, readings for student preparation.	Receives case and reading assignments.
	Prepares for class. Completes Case Teaching Plan.	Reads and prepares individually. Starts the Case Preparation Chart.
	(May consult with colleagues about the case.)	Participates in a small group discussion of the case. Adds to the Case Preparation Chart.
During Class	Resolves questions arising out of the assigned readings.	Raises questions regarding assigned readings.
	Leads the case discussion by questioning, recording and facilitating student comments, supplying data, theory or insight which may enhance the thinking and learning in the class. Executes the Case Teaching Plan	Participates in the class discussion by sharing insights on the case and listens carefully to what others have to say. Uses the Case Preparation Chart.
After Class	Evaluates the participation of students and records impressions.	Reviews class results in light of preparation.
	Evaluates the Case Teaching Plan.	Reviews the Case Preparation Chart.
	Evaluates the case and other materials in light of the original teaching objectives and updates teaching notes.	Notes key learning points.

Learning with Cases, the companion book, is focused on the student or participant role in the case method. It explains why cases are used and what the case method is all about. The core of *Learning with Cases* contains detailed suggestions for students on how to prepare a case individually, discuss it in a small group and in a class. Also covered are case presentations, reports and exams, and effective management of the learning process.

The Case Difficulty Cube (see Exhibit 1-2), the Three Stage Learning Process (see Exhibit 1-3), and the Case Preparation Chart (see Exhibit 1-4), explained in *Learning with Cases,* provide conceptual ways of thinking about the

Exhibit 1–2
THE CASE DIFFICULTY CUBE

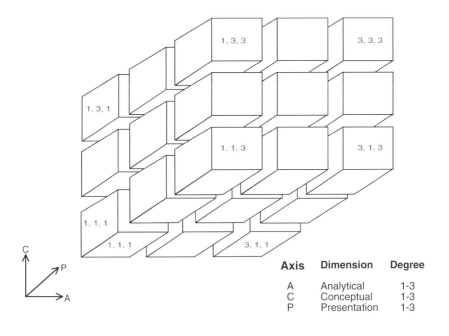

Axis	Dimension	Degree
A	Analytical	1-3
C	Conceptual	1-3
P	Presentation	1-3

case learning process and serve as useful basic tools. In short, *Learning with Cases* raises the bar on student preparation and participation. By applying the principles of re-engineering and focusing on the value-adding activities in the learning process, the authors have simplified the learning task, improved the output, and limited the time required for students to prepare and participate effectively. The net outcome is higher quality learning and more enjoyment during a shortened learning process.

Exhibit 1–3
THE THREE STAGE LEARNING PROCESS

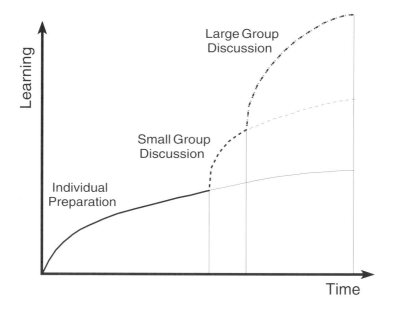

Exhibit 1–4
CASE PREPARATION CHART

Case Title:					*Case Assignment:*

**I.	SHORT CYCLE PROCESS**

        Name   Position

Who:

        Issue(s)

What:

Why:

When:

        Case Difficulty Cube

How: (_____, _____, _____)
      Analytical, Conceptual, Presentation

**II.	LONG CYCLE PROCESS**

  **A.	Issue(s)**

Immediate					Basic

1.						1.
2.						2.
3.						3.

  **B.	Case Data Analysis**

**II.	LONG CYCLE PROCESS (continued)**

  **C.	Alternative Generation**

    1.
    2.
    3.

  **D.	Decision Criteria**

    1.
    2.
    3.

  **E.	Alternative Assessment**

Quantitative	+			N			–		
Qualitative	+	N	–	+	N	–	+	N	–
Decision	go	go	?	?	no	no	?	no	no

  **F.	Preferred Alternative**

    Predicted Outcome

  **G.	Action & Implementation Plan**

                           Timing
                          Milestones
    Who
    What
    When
    Where
    How

    Missing Information

    Assumptions

Reference: *Learning with Cases*, 2001, page 36

The goals in *Teaching with Cases* are similar for teachers. Quality case teaching requires extensive preparation, careful thinking, and a tremendous personal commitment. This text intends to give both new and experienced case teachers an organized perspective on the teaching task, as well as time saving and effectiveness improving suggestions. It ties in directly with the key concepts advanced in *Learning with Cases* and adds the Case Teaching Plan as a simple device to keep the instructor focused.

Our suggestion is that readers start with *Learning with Cases*. It is an easy and fast read and, since an instructor's class preparation starts at exactly the same point as a normal participant's, *Learning with Cases* is a prerequisite to *Teaching with Cases*. Moreover, thorough understanding of how students are supposed to learn with cases is fundamental to being able to teach with the case method. Rather than repeating everything from *Learning with Cases* in this case teaching text, we decided to put the two together as a complementary set.

Some ideas advanced in *Learning with Cases* will be reinforced in this text. For the sake of brevity, however, this book will not discuss cases and the case method and all of the other topics covered in the companion book. Instead, it will focus on the exclusive domain of the instructor in the case method. Exhibit 1-5 provides a quick overview of how *Learning with Cases* and *Teaching with Cases* are integrated.

Exhibit 1-5
THE INTEGRATION OF *LEARNING WITH CASES* AND *TEACHING WITH CASES*

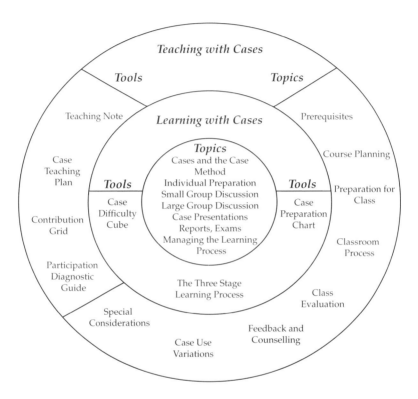

NEED FOR INFORMATION CONCERNING TEACHING WITH CASES

"I don't know what I'm supposed to do." Almost every person new to teaching with cases says this to anyone who is willing to listen. Frequently, it is difficult to find sympathetic ears. Some people who know how to teach with cases have learned the hard way. "You sink or swim." Many are convinced it is the only way to learn. As long as the use of cases was largely restricted to a few North American schools, "sink or swim" was acceptable. The use of cases is no longer an educational elitist process, but a practical answer to some of education's most basic challenges. It allows the student to: (1) participate in discussing the analysis and solution of relevant and practical problems; (2) apply theory to practice, instead of learning by memory; and (3) learn by doing and teaching others. Furthermore, it allows the faculty member to work with students as a learning facilitator and not as an oracle.

The use of cases continues to grow and has spread geographically to almost all parts of the world. The case method is also used in engineering, social sciences, medicine, education, economics, mathematics, law, computer and actuarial sciences, hospitality and recreation, agriculture, nursing, theology, and other educational areas. Part-time and in-house development programs increasingly use cases as well as executive programs. This growing interest in the case method reinforces the need for information sharing about case writing, learning and teaching; and has increased the demand for competent educators.

Today's students, young or old, are leaning towards participatory education and are no longer satisfied to be passive recipients of knowledge. The educational process itself is becoming an important consideration and must be satisfying to its consumers. That is, the topic may draw students to a course, the process of learning will retain them. How to make the educational process interesting to an audience continually exposed to some of the world's most sophisticated entertainment on audio-visual media is not an easy challenge for today's teacher.

TERMINOLOGY

In this text a *teacher*, instructor, lecturer, professor, facilitator, faculty member, educator, case leader, trainer or moderator is someone who has program, course, class, seminar or workshop instruction responsibility. A *student*, participant or class member is someone who is part of a group taking a course, seminar, workshop or educational program. The terms have been used interchangeably to avoid monotony and will be clear in their context.

A *case* is a description of an actual situation, commonly involving a decision, a challenge, an opportunity, a problem or an issue faced by a person, or persons, in an organization. A case is based on actual field data, authenticated by a release. It is not of the armchair or fictional variety.

The normal assumption in this book is that the case will appear in print form, as opposed to other formats such as film, videotape or CD ROM, since the hard copy case remains the most common type because of cost and convenience.

This text will focus on teaching in a classroom with face-to-face interaction, as opposed to using video conferencing or the Internet.

The Case Method

The term "case method" often means different things to different people.

We suggest that there are four potential sources of semantic difficulty. These may be revealed through the following questions: (1) What is included in the case method? (2) Does the case method require one specific teaching style? (3) Does the case method require a minimum number of cases? (4) Is the context of the case method course, program, or institution based?

1. What is included in the case method? A significant part of the ambiguity surrounding the case method seems to lie in the question whether the case method itself incorporates the use of other educational philosophies and techniques. For example, can someone be teaching by the case method and still use lectures, problems, exercises, experiential learning, problem-based learning, project-oriented and collaborative learning, simulations, games, films, field trips, reports or any other teaching/learning technique? Yes, of course, this is not only possible but it is also highly beneficial to provide diversity of learning experiences. However, we believe it is appropriate to call it the case method if a significant percentage of all the class time in a course is devoted to case discussion.

2. Does the case method require one specific teaching style? The myth of the non-directive instructor, passive or impassive, is widespread. Under this myth, the responsibility for learning rests solely on the student's shoulders. Any interference from the instructor is seen as a violation of the whole learning process.

In reality, we observe that most instructors prefer to adopt a more active role in the classroom. The case method does not restrict a teacher to one teaching style only

3. Does the case method require a minimum number of cases? Some instructors claim to be using the case method when they use only one or two cases per year in their course. Does this constitute using the case method? Generally speaking, we believe, if there is such a thing as "the case method," it involves a higher rather than a lower percentage of cases taught.

4. Is the context of the case method course, program, or institution based? Thus far, the assumption has been that the context for the case method is a course. Some people hold that the case method can only be taught in a program context. Therefore, unless a reasonable number of courses in a program are taught using a significant percentage of cases in each course, there can be no case method.

Advocates of the program context argue that there is a synergistic effect which must be shared by all teachers in the program for the case method to work effectively. Anything short of such a cooperative approach is not likely to result in "the case method." A program may include undergraduate, graduate or executive development. It could be a number of years in length, or be as short as a few days.

A further extension leads to the institutional context. It might be possible to take all the institutions in the world teaching management, for example, and determine in which of those a significant number of courses or programs are taught using cases. In reality, such institutions exist and they are often called case method schools. One source of confusion for people not familiar with what transpires inside these schools is the assumption that 100% of class time is devoted to case discussion. Another source of confusion for the people within these same schools originates from the use of many educational techniques other than the case method. They argue that, "Because we are labelled a case method school, and I see us using every teaching method imaginable, the case method must include all of these."

Some believers in the case method hold that the only way the case method can possibly be taught is if the institution: (1) is involved in the writing of new cases; (2) has physical accommodation for effective class discussion and small group discussions; (3) schedules for adequate individual preparation and small group discussion; and (4) recognizes the teaching and development of cases as significant academic contributions.

Even for these people, the question remains as to what degree cases should be used to achieve the objectives of the institution, the program and the course.

TEACHING WITH CASES

Since the case method clearly means different things to different people, we have chosen the title "Teaching with Cases" for this book, as our way of reaching all users of cases. The purpose of this text is to assist anyone interested in teaching with cases. Our assumption will be that to be teaching with cases, someone has to use a minimum of one case in a course. Our assumption will also be that it is possible to use the case method on an individual course basis. We recognize that some of the benefits of the case method may not exist in an institution where only one course is taught with a minimum percentage of cases. We also recognize that it is possible to make a program or institutional commitment to the case method. We prefer to reserve the term teaching with cases for the total set of activities related to the use of cases in the classroom. We prefer to call a problem discussion, a film, a lecture, a simulation, a business game, a class discussion, a question and answer period, a field trip, a student presentation, a reading, and any other educational technique by its proper name.

Class Size

Should there be a minimum number of students in class before an instructor can reasonably use cases? Similarly, is there an upper limit to class size beyond which case discussion becomes inoperable? The principle that guides the answers to these questions is the meaningful involvement of a maximum number of students in a given period of time. It is to some extent a function not only of class length but also of the number of classes. The longer the class time and the higher the percentage of case classes in a course, the larger the number of students in the class can be. Generally, the lower bound lies close to a dozen and the upper near a hundred participants while the ideal case class probably varies from twenty to sixty.

ORGANIZATION AND PRESENTATION OF THE MATERIAL

This text is organized so that the central core covers the chronological sequence of preparation for class, in-class teaching and evaluation after class. Other topics, such as prerequisites, course planning, and feedback and counseling surround this core. The beginning instructor, faced with taking over an existing course which already uses some cases, may wish to concentrate on the prerequisites, preparation for class, classroom process and evaluation chapters. Those not so fortunate as to have the course pre-planned for them may wish to add course planning. For the more experienced case teacher, case use variations, special considerations and the conclusion will add further insights to augment his or her experience.

Chapter 2 presents prerequisites, the essential basic building blocks for effective case teaching.

Chapter 3 on course planning introduces the kinds of challenges involved in determining objectives, selecting cases and conceptual/theoretical materials, and defining performance evaluation measures.

Chapter 4 covers instructor preparation for a case class. Experienced case teachers recognize the importance and necessity of thorough preparation for every class. However, new instructors are sometimes surprised to learn of the extensive preparation time required for a case class. The aim of this chapter is to complement the student Case Preparation Chart in *Learning with Cases*.

Chapter 5 focuses on the teaching of a case class. It is here that the results of planning and preparation will show. Starting from a reference base class description, a number of variations and practices are discussed. The normal chronological parts of a case class are identified, followed by sections on questioning and responding, managing the participative process, and dealing with participation problems.

Chapter 6 addresses evaluation after class. This evaluation includes participant evaluation, Case Teaching Plan review, material evaluation, personal evaluation, class assessment, and teaching note review.

Chapter 7, on feedback and counseling, helps instructors deal with student performance issues. This chapter also discusses case exams, as well as course evaluation and instructor feedback.

Chapter 8 covers several aspects of the use of cases that, while not necessarily used on a daily basis, are, nonetheless, effective. Case use variations include: case presentations, case reports, role plays, case format variations, visitors to class, team teaching and field trips.

Chapter 9 is devoted to special considerations and covers subjects which did not neatly fall under any of the earlier headings, including teacher training, managing diversity, shortcuts used by students, and using cases in a non-case environment.

Chapter 10 concludes with an operations perspective on the challenges of teaching with cases.

CONCLUSION

Throughout this text it will be apparent that there are different ways of dealing with the challenges inherent in the case method. Every teacher needs to find his or her own "comfort zone." The case method offers a variety of options in executing the teaching task. The challenge is to find a way of teaching that is appropriate to the subject, the participants and the teacher as well. We are fully convinced that there are fundamentals to the case teaching process. These include paying attention to the prerequisites, proper course planning and preparation before class; being able to conduct the class according to a plan and congruent with one's own personality; consistent evaluation and feedback; and the right mix of rigor, humor and variety. These fundamentals will go a long way to ensuring teaching effectiveness. Hard work and willingness to experiment do have their payoffs. Few case teachers have such a scintillating charisma and outstanding intellect that they can short-cut the full set of tasks required to assure success.

This text has been used in a high number of case teaching training programs. These experiences have shown that many teachers find it useful to learn about teaching with cases from others. The "mystique" of teaching with cases can be removed. It is reassuring for the new case teacher to know that others have faced similar problems. Some of the more elementary pitfalls may be avoided. We have tried to illustrate in this text the variety and richness inherent in the use of cases with a deep concern for student excitement in the learning process.

prerequisites for teaching with cases

In the first chapter of our book *Learning with* Cases, we provide an exhaustive rationale for the use of cases in the classroom and an inventory of the various skills developed by the case method. It is one step to make an intellectual commitment to this philosophy of learning. The participative nature of the case method actually requires a deeper understanding of what makes its effectiveness a reality. It all begins with a commitment to set-up time and effort. In the first place, physical facilities must be conducive to the use of cases. The layout of the classroom must encourage participation. Secondly, means must be provided whereby the teacher can learn quickly the names of the participants and for the participants to become acquainted with one another. There is no room for anonymity in the case method! Lastly, materials must be available. Students must have the cases in order to prepare for the class. Failure to attend to these prerequisites or unwillingness to spend the time necessary to assure that they are fulfilled may well result in an unsatisfactory experience in teaching with cases. This chapter will present these three prerequisites individually: physical facilities, participant identification and material logistics.

PHYSICAL FACILITIES

Classroom Physical Layout

A proper physical layout for a classroom is extremely important in using cases. The basic principle behind a proper physical layout is simply that all participants, including the instructor, must be able to hear and see each other easily in class. If the instructor is unable to identify a student who is talking and if students are unable to identify and face other students who are contributing to the discussion, major blocks exist to effective participation. Since it is likely that educators will find themselves in classrooms not originally designed for using cases, a few comments are in order regarding physical layout.

The traditional classroom in most universities and educational institutions (or seminar room in hotels) is designed as follows: A rectangular room is set up with a podium or desk and board at the narrow end of the room and rows of seats and benches facing that end of the room. (See Exhibit 2-1.) For one-way communication such as a lecture where the primary task of the student is to listen to the speaker, such an arrangement is functional. It may not be the best, because it is often difficult to see or hear the speaker from the back.

From the point of view of teaching with cases, this layout has many difficulties. Since case discussion requires two-way communication, it is difficult for a student in the back row to talk to the backs of the heads of the people in the front rows. It is also difficult for those at the front to turn around and see the student contributing from the back of the room. As far as using cases is concerned, this layout places an undue emphasis on the teacher or instructor and not enough on the participants.

Exhibit 2-1
TRADITIONAL CLASSROOM LAYOUT

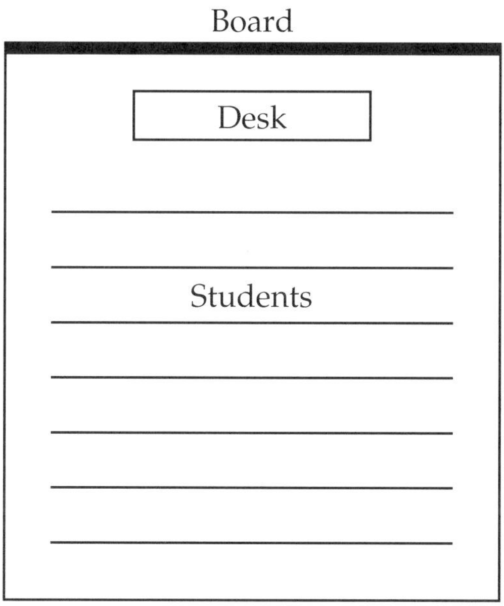

Board

Desk

Students

The ideal layout for using cases with a small number of participants would be a perfectly round table and a circular seating arrangement. (See Exhibit 2-2.) The circle implies equality for all participants, provides perfect sight lines to everyone and allows face-to-face communication.

Other variations exist on the circle theme. For example, it is possible to use a square or a rectangular layout. Actually, a hexagon or octagon are preferable to either the square or the rectangle because both improve sight lines to participants. (See Exhibit 2-3.)

Exhibit 2-2
IDEAL ARRANGEMENT FOR
SMALL CLASS CASE DISCUSSIONS

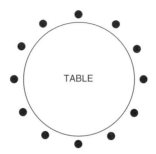

Exhibit 2-3
VARIATIONS ON THE CIRCLE OPTION

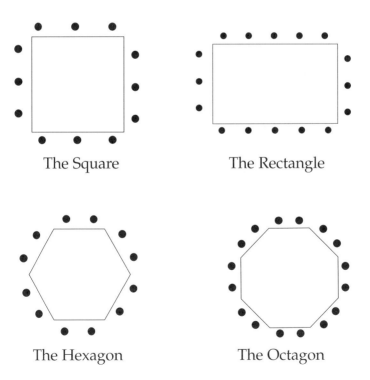

The Square   The Rectangle

The Hexagon   The Octagon

Unfortunately, as the number of participants increases, the circle and its variations start to have disadvantages. There is a limit to the size of the table. The distance between participants grows rapidly as their number increases. The amount of useless space in the middle of the table becomes a block to communication.

For larger groups, other options need to be examined. Various arrangements of row seating, preferably ramped, in amphitheater style are possible alternatives. (See Exhibits 2-4 and 2-5.) Chairs should be moveable or at least rotatable, so that participants in the front can easily turn around and see people behind them. Table or bench space in front of each participant is desirable both for comfort and as a place to put cases and reference materials, lap tops or to take notes. These should provide for slightly more depth than a normal written case. About 14 inches or 35 centimeters is adequate. Curved benches (see Exhibit 2-5) are preferable to long straight benches (see Exhibit 2-4). The curve helps make it easier to see others seated in the same row.

To preserve sight lines it is necessary to make each additional row at a substantially higher level than the previous ones (see Exhibit 2-5). For this reason, there is a practical limit to how many rows can be accommodated in one classroom. The maximum is normally four or five rows.

Sometimes it is possible to use small tables in a room and seat participants around these tables. Frequently, this is an effective setup in a hotel for short seminars. The group around the table can form a discussion group at the same time. (See Exhibits 2-6 and 2-7.)

Exhibit 2-4
BENCH AND CHAIR ARRANGEMENTS

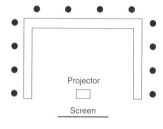

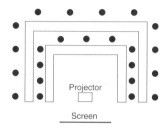

1. Simple Straight U   2. Double Straight U

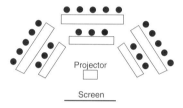

3. Double Angled U

Exhibit 2-5
CURVED BENCH AND CHAIR ARRANGEMENT

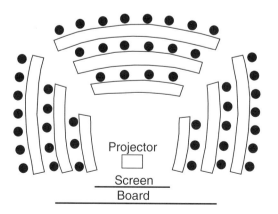

Side view showing increasing ramp height with each additional row of seating

Exhibit 2-6
POSSIBLE LAYOUT USING ROUND TABLES

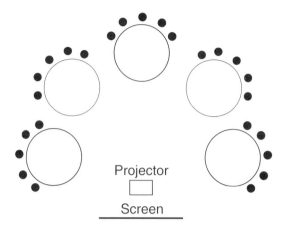

Exhibit 2-7
POSSIBLE LAYOUT USING RECTANGULAR TABLES

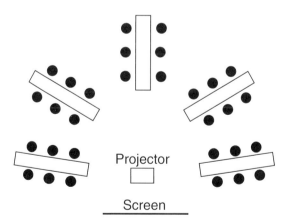

Most "case schools" have classrooms designed especially for the case method. Appendix 1, at the end of the book, contains proven and effective case classroom designs for rooms of 44 and 71 participants.

Adjusting to Non-Ideal Environments

A number of schools have experimented successfully with changing traditional classrooms (see Exhibit 2-1) to a more discussion oriented design (see Exhibit 2-8). One option is to move the (black, green or white) board from the short wall in a traditional lecture room to the long wall. Adding two more boards, including one in the corner, is a second option.

Exhibit 2-8
TRADITIONAL CLASSROOM
CONVERSION OPTIONS

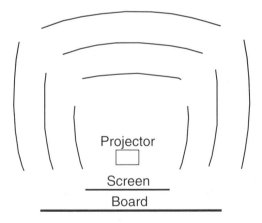

Option 1
Conversion from Exhibit 2-1 with Board on Long Wall

Exhibit 2-8 (continued)

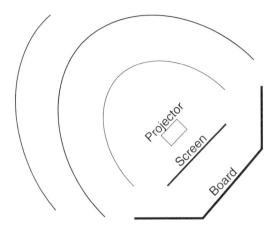

Option 2
Conversion from Exhibit 2-1 with Boards in Corner

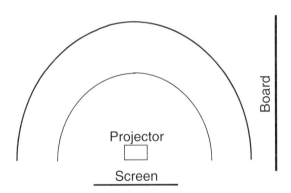

Option 3
Simple Temporary Conversion from
Exhibit 2-1 by Moving Chairs

It is even possible as a third option to take individual student chairs, provided they are not bolted to the floor, and move them in some broad semicircles. With a screen and overhead projector, this can be done even if no board is available on the long wall.

Sometimes the room available is too large for the number of class members. This in itself can create a communication obstacle. The instructor should insist on participants sitting close to create a sense of unity.

If the room is too small for the number of students and no larger room is available, breaking the class into two or more sections may be required.

Instructors who are used to the luxury of an "ideal" case classroom find it difficult at times to adjust to new surroundings when they are teaching away from home, especially in hotels. It is often very hard to get staff to set up the room in a configuration so that everybody can see each other. It is therefore imperative for the instructor to check the room ahead of time and make necessary changes to the seating arrangements. It is also important to clear the space in front of the room, removing furnishings that physically separate the instructor from the participants, except for a table for the instructor's materials.

Even if everything has been set properly, it is always useful to get the "feel" of a classroom before the first class, to know its layout, so as to see how the instructor can move and walk around comfortably.

Boards, Charts and Screens

The participatory nature of case class discussion also requires boards, charts or screens to facilitate the discussion by providing a visual record.

Traditionally, classrooms have been equipped with blackboards that instructors have used to document and keep track of the discussion. Over the years, these blackboards have turned green, blue or white and become superimposed with sliding mechanisms. The messy chalk has disappeared to be replaced by colorful erasable markers used on white boards. Increasingly, these various types of recording boards or flip-charts, common in facilities not equipped with boards, are supplemented or simply replaced by projectors which have the great advantage of allowing the instructor to face the participants instead of turning his or her back to them. With the advent of new technologies and the electronic classroom, the nature of recording mechanisms keeps evolving.

Prior to class it is also useful to check the projection equipment, the availability of board or flip-chart accessories, and the lighting. In the modern classroom, control consoles are provided to enable the instructor to use electronic devices and adjust lighting and sound appropriately.

Small Group Facilities

Another concern is the availability of space for small group or learning team discussion. As described in *Learning with Cases*, small group discussion provides the vital link between individual preparation and large group discussion in the Three Stage Case Learning Process. Yet space and time for enabling this important stage of learning is often left for participants to arrange.

While some flexibility exists with respect to meeting space for such groups because of their small size, it remains important for institutions to provide small rooms, preferably equipped with boards, that may be booked ahead of time. The availability of these rooms, while reinforcing the importance of small group discussion, will prove especially convenient to participants enrolled in evening or part-time programs, who do not have regular contact with each other, or to participants of in-house programs.

While not ideal, the instructor can sometimes use the large classroom for the purpose of small group discussion, when separate rooms are not available.

It is easy to underestimate the impact of suitable physical arrangements on the effectiveness of the case learning process. Anyone seriously contemplating using cases in class must first make sure that the physical facilities can be satisfactorily arranged. Considerable instructor ingenuity may have to be used to satisfy this first prerequisite to effective case use.

PARTICIPANT IDENTIFICATION

"Will the person with the glasses at the end of the row mind starting the class?"

"Will you, second in from the left in the third row, please tell me what you think?"

"Will the person with a beard wearing a yellow shirt comment on this?"

To dedicated case teachers these kinds of comments are totally unacceptable in a well-run case class. It is the responsibility of the instructor to get to know his or her students as quickly as possible. This means being able to identify each participant by name in and out of class. It also means having background information, if possible, on each participant. In case discussions a student is not a number. A student is not anonymous. A student cannot be allowed to hide in the classroom. It is the responsibility of both the instructor and the students to get to know everyone in the class. For this purpose a number of aids are normally available. The more common ones are listed below:

1. Personal data forms. Personal data forms on all participants are a very useful starting point for student identification. Personal data can be obtained during registration or in the early stages of starting the course. A copy of a typical personal data form is shown in Exhibit 2-9.

2. Seat cards. Seat cards, also called place cards, are a great identifying aid. They are placed in the classroom in front of each participant's seat. They can be made of paper or plastic and can be of the "quick and dirty" variety or the very professional type. Legibility is crucial. The simplest ones are rectangular pieces of heavy paper or cardboard folded in two. Seat cards can be collected by the instructor after class or left for the participants to bring back each class.

For executive programs, sometimes company affiliation is shown on the seat card in addition to the first and last names of the participant. It is useful to write on both sides of the seat card so that people sitting behind the speaker know who is talking. (See Exhibit 2-10 for typical classroom seat card options.)

Exhibit 2–9
PERSONAL DATA FORM

MBA STUDENT BIOGRAPHY

(Please do not attach extra sheets or write on the back of this form)

Mr. ☐ Ms. ☐

Name _____
 Surname   First   Second

Name to be used by professors and classsmates _____

Marital status _____ Spouse's name _____ No. of children _____

Age as of September 15th this year _____

What field are you interested in pursuing upon graduation? _____

Please indicate your reasons for pursuing the MBA Program _____
_____
_____

Place of Birth _____ Student Status: Canadian ☐   Landed Immigrant ☐   Visa

First Language _____ Other languages fluently spoken _____
IINTERNATIONAL EXPERIENCE:

Education: Country _____ Duration: _____

Employment: Country _____ Duration: _____

Travel: Country _____ Duration: _____

EDUCATION

University	Location	From	To	Degree Awarded	Major

EMPLOYMENT

Estimate the total amount of full time work experience by the time you enter the MBA Program.   Years _____   Months _____

Employer	Location	Job Title	Dates of Employment (M/Yr. - M/Yr.)

EXTRA-CURRICULAR ACTIVITIES (include non-academic interests)

Activ:ties/Interests/Hobbies	Location	Position Held	Dates

Exhibit 2-10
TYPICAL CLASSROOM SEAT CARD OPTIONS

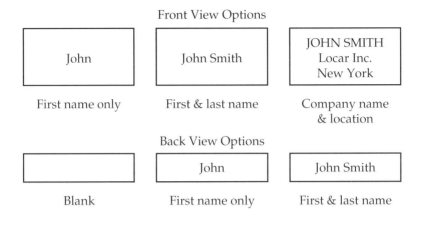

Front View Options

John	John Smith	JOHN SMITH Locar Inc. New York
First name only	First & last name	Company name & location

Back View Options

	John	John Smith
Blank	First name only	First & last name

Seat Card Holder Options

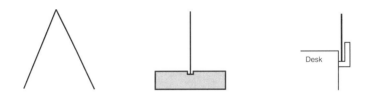

Desk

3. Name tags. Name tags, hanging around the neck or attached to the clothing, are useful to identify participants while they are not sitting in class. In executive and management programs, name tags are likely to be worn for the total length of the program.

4. Personal introductions in class. Having each student introduce him or herself during the first class of a course or program reinforces the idea that, "In this course everyone is important and everyone is expected to speak in class."

5. *Photos.* There are two types of photos which may be useful in identifying participants. Individual photos can be requested at the time of registration. Sometimes, the quality of these can vary substantially as well as the age. Human rights laws also may make the obtaining of photos difficult. Classroom photos showing every participant in their place are of substantial assistance to get an up-to-date picture. They have the advantage of identifying for both the instructor and the students a current picture and class layout in combination. It is a good idea to place a picture of this kind in the classroom so that students themselves can refer to it. Ideally, if every student can receive a copy, so much the better. Digital cameras make it possible to e-mail class photos to each participant. When the services of a professional photographer cannot be retained, using one's own camera is always an option.

6. *Layout sheets or seating charts.* It is a simple matter for the instructor to pass a classroom layout sheet around the room and ask every student to fill in his or her name. This can subsequently be cleaned up, copied and passed around to everyone. (See Exhibit 2-11.)

All of the above means are clear and graphic indications to the student that individual identification is of high priority. The professor can take the following further steps to assist in participant identification.

7. *Sitting in the back of the class.* For certain programs it may be possible to sit in the back of the class when another instructor is teaching. It is possible then to observe every student and mark down individual characteristics on a layout sheet to help in participant identification. Experience has shown that it is possible to identify a group of 60 in approximately 80 minutes.

Exhibit 2–11
TYPICAL CLASSROOM LAYOUT SHEET

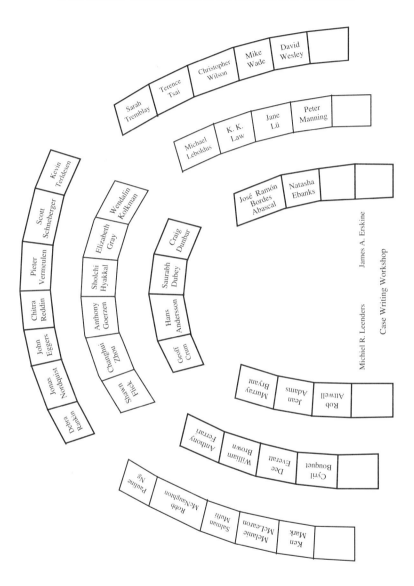

8. *Participation in social activities.* Further participant identification is possible during coffee breaks, lunch, social functions and other gatherings at which students and instructors can mingle.

9. *Personal visits in the office.* A student's visit to a teacher's office allows both to know each other better.

10. *Small group visits.* In programs that provide space and mechanisms to organize small groups formally, it is possible for the instructor to visit the groups and identify students. Such visits have the added advantage of reinforcing the value of small groups. (See Chapter 4 in *Learning with Cases.*)

It is normal to use a combination of the above means to assist in student identification.

A Typical Participant Identification Routine in Case Schools

In case schools a typical routine to acquaint professors with students is: Before classes start, the school organizes a reception for new students who wear name tags. Faculty have a chance to meet a number of their students informally at this occasion.

Each professor is also assigned an advisee group of students. During the first few days of school, the instructor makes a point of meeting with the members of this group individually or as a whole.

Seat cards can be pre-arranged alphabetically in the classroom or by other decision rules recognizing gender, culture or experience. Alternatively, students can choose their own seat location.

Personal data forms with a picture of each student are made available to instructors before the beginning of the school term.

Seating Arrangements and Data on Participants

Most case programs have fixed seating arrangements with permanent place cards, which greatly facilitate the evaluation of participation and noting of absences. Some professors are even used to an alphabetical class layout which conforms to the arrangement of the personal data forms. Many programs allow the participants to change place two to four times over the year. For the professor who likes to think of the class as an orchestra, lack of seating continuity can be a disaster. What would happen to the maestro if the violin section kept moving to a different location for every concert? If it is not possible to have permanent seating arrangements, the instructor should insist that the students always carry their seat cards and display them in each class.

It is also useful to know the background of all participants. The personal data forms can assist the instructor in preparing for and conducting the class. Whom to call on and in what order can be important. A participant may have a background that relates to a specific case. The instructor can use the information to find who are the "experts," such as lawyer, banker or engineer, to call on during particular sessions. It is therefore advisable to get to know students quickly to be able to work with all the experiences that the participants bring to the class.

Even on very short courses, workshops or seminars, instructors should make a serious attempt to become acquainted with all participants. A good way to start is by asking every participant to introduce himself or herself. The instructor can make seat cards, if not provided, and a rough seating chart during the introductions. While participants are busy in individual preparation or small group discussion, it is possible to learn their names. This will certainly pay off for the rest of the program.

The process of getting to know the group may be difficult and may require a lot of work for some teachers, but it is worth the effort. Without participant identification it is impossible to conduct an effective case class. It is important that the student senses that he or she belongs. The student must feel a responsibility to self and the group. The student must also know that the instructor cares.

Knowing the students is also necessary for evaluative purposes. The instructor can only grade class participation in a credible fashion if he or she knows who's who. Students will also get a clear message that they cannot hide in class.

Moreover, a professor demonstrating good knowledge of each participant can gain valuable student support. Students are visibly impressed when they are called by their own name during their early days in the course. "How come you know my name?" is a frequent comment on their part.

Just like a suitable physical layout, proper student identification is key to effective communication and, therefore, an essential prerequisite.

MATERIAL LOGISTICS

The assumption behind using cases is that cases will be available for use. In the so-called "case schools," reproduction facilities and ordering procedures are usually geared to create a minimum of fuss and bother to assure case access to students.

The European Case Clearing House (ECCH) provides through its Case On Line Information System (COLIS) the most comprehensive electronic bibliography of business cases in the world. COLIS contains abstracts of cases and supplementary materials from the major case producing management schools of the world (see Appendix 2) in addition to information on cases submitted by individuals.

In North America, the best known source of cases remains the Harvard Business School Publishing Division. It publishes a number of bibliographies which comprise several thousand case studies, including teaching notes, case videos and a selection of software ancillaries. The Richard Ivey School of Business at The University of Western Ontario is the second largest producer of cases in the world and is the main source of cases in Canada. Harvard and Ivey have an update system designed to inform faculty by e-mail about new cases on a subject specific basis. Harvard and Ivey also have watermarked copies of selected cases on their website which can be downloaded for inspection free of charge to registered academics. Appendix 2 presents a list of the major case distribution centres of the world.

Lead time for ordering cases will vary depending on size of the order, location of user, location of source, and time of year. How students are to pay for case materials can apparently be tricky in some institutions and may well be a nuisance barrier to the use of cases. Some instructors find it easier to adopt a casebook from a commercial publisher. While a casebook may simplify matters from a price and logistics point of view, it may lessen the flexibility to make course adjustments.

While access to cases has been simplified greatly with the advent of new communication technologies, it is still not always easy to acquire relevant case material for student use. Because of copyright regulations, instructors cannot change anything in existing cases to suit their needs.

The Internet facilitates access not only to cases but also to teaching notes, peer support and other curriculum resources. For example, eligible instructors can subscribe to services that will give them access to full-text files of cases and teaching notes to view on-screen or to download and print. Instructors can also join various case discussion groups or associations such as the North American Case Research Association (NACRA) and the World Association for Case Research and Application (WACRA), to participate in professional activities, to share expertise and experiences, and to learn from colleagues from around the world.

Instructors can also write their own cases. Each year the Richard Ivey School of Business offers a Case Writing Workshop in the third week in April and a Case Teaching Workshop the last week in August for anyone interested from around the world (see http://www.ivey.uwo.ca /workshops.) Our book *Writing Cases* provides a proven approach to quick and effective case writing and has been used by thousands of instructors in workshops throughout the world.

Chapter 3 on course planning will offer further insights on case selection and the difficulties of finding good case materials.

CONCLUSION

Teaching with cases requires a commitment to the three prerequisites. Making sure the physical facilities are conducive to small and large group discussion is the first major step. The second is get to know the class participants quickly. Thirdly, case materials must be available on time. Simple as these prerequisites may seem, they could create serious stumbling blocks without adequate attention.

course planning

Course planning using cases is not all that different in the broadest sense from non-case course planning. The four common parts to the course planning process are: (1) setting the learning objectives; (2) the general course design; (3) detailed planning - sequencing of the sessions and materials; and (4) defining the performance evaluation measures. The special aspect of using cases raises parallel questions such as: (1) Which of the learning objectives require cases? (2) How many cases will be used as a percentage of all class sessions? (3) What specific cases are to be used and where in the course? Will they be used to introduce the need for theory, concepts, tools and techniques or will they be used later to give practice in application? (4) What percentage of the course grade will be credited to case work and how will case work be assessed?

SETTING THE LEARNING OBJECTIVES

Learning by doing and learning by teaching others are the two fundamentals of teaching with cases that permeate the learning objectives in case course planning. Courses that do not use cases typically have learning objectives tied to the conceptual dimension of the Case Difficulty Cube. For example: "Students must be able to identify the major theoretical constructs in the field and explain the key differences between them."

The use of cases and the analytical and presentation dimensions of the Case Difficulty Cube add a list of additional learning objectives. Decision making, communication, information handling and time management skills can be perceived more as life versus academic skills. They tend to be non-course specific and thus tie in to school or program philosophy and intent. Instructors keen on using cases must face up to the reality that trade-offs are unavoidable, especially when student preparation and class time are fixed. It is not possible to assign the same amount of theoretical reading in a case course as is possible in a non-case course. A serious cost-benefit analysis is inherent in any case course design. The course designer has to be fully aware of the trade-off decisions made and the reasons for them.

The following sections identify the potential learning objectives inherent in the use of cases. First, the objectives will be tied to the Case Difficulty Cube as discussed in Chapter 2 of *Learning with Cases*. Learning objectives will also be addressed as part of the Three Stage Learning Process also discussed in Chapter 2 of *Learning with Cases*. Next, learning objectives will be related to the Case Preparation Chart discussed in Chapter 3 of *Learning with Cases*. Learning objectives are also connected to the eight participant skills developed through case use reviewed in Chapter 1 in *Learning with Cases*.

Learning Objectives and the Case Difficulty Cube

Learning objectives for cases can be connected to the Case Difficulty Cube by focusing on the three dimensions of difficulty and the degrees within each dimension as summarized in Exhibit 3-1.

In summary, it can be seen that the primary challenge in the analytical dimension is the participant's ability to apply the decision making process to a situation. Under the conceptual dimension, it is the participant's ability to apply relevant theory and concepts, tools and techniques, in an appropriate way to a specific decision. In the presentation dimension, it is the ability to deal with complexity, ambiguity, incompleteness of data, as well as information sorting, specifying, organizing and prioritizing.

Exhibit 3-1
LEARNING OBJECTIVES
AND THE CASE DIFFICULTY CUBE

ANALYTICAL DIMENSION
Difficulty 1 The student must be able to evaluate a decision taken by others; assess the appropriateness of the decision to the problem or issue identified, whether the appropriate alternatives have been considered and the appropriate decision criteria applied; suggest other alternatives, should the ones offered in the case be deemed inadequate; and develop an appropriate action and implementation plan.
Difficulty 2 The student must be able to assess the issue, decision or opportunity identified on an importance and urgency matrix; assess causes and effects where appropriate; develop alternatives and decision criteria and select the alternative that best fits the quantitative and qualitative assessment of them; develop an action and implementation plan; and specify missing information.
Difficulty 3 The participant must be able to assess the situation and identify problems, issues and challenges. From here the learning objectives are the same as under Difficulty 2.

Exhibit 3–1 (continued)

CONCEPTUAL DIMENSION

Difficulty 1
A participant should be able to apply a single, simple theory or concept to a specific case problem or issue without requiring extra explanation of the theory or concept in class.

Difficulty 2
The participant should be able to apply the appropriate theory or concepts or a single complex concept with some assistance or further discussion and explanation in class.

Difficulty 3
The participant should be able to apply a variety of those theories and concepts which might be relevant to the case issues. The participant may require a substantial amount of assistance and explanation in class to understand the integration of these theories or the explanation of the complex theories which are part of the total set.

PRESENTATION DIMENSION

Difficulty 1
The participant should be able to analyze correctly a short, well-organized case, containing no extraneous information, little missing relevant information and presented in a single format.

Difficulty 2
The participant should be able to analyze correctly a medium length case with some disorganization, containing a medium amount of extraneous information, with some missing information and presented in a single format.

Difficulty 3
The participant should be able to analyze within a reasonable length of time a long case which may be disorganized, containing lots of extraneous information, a substantial amount of missing information and presented in a variety of formats.

Learning Objectives and
the Three Stage Learning Process

Learning objectives can also be connected to the Three Stage Learning Process.

Stage 1 - Individual Preparation

The participant has to learn how to read and prepare a case on his or her own using the information provided, apply the Short and Long Cycle Processes of analysis, and prepare a Case Preparation Chart in a period of less than two hours. The participant has to learn to work independently, and develop self-confidence, time management and critical thinking skills. The participant has to learn to recognize what constitutes satisfactory preparation for the next stage: small group discussion.

Stage 2 - Small Group Discussion

The participant must be able to contribute his or her ideas to the small group discussion dealing with any topic on the Case Preparation Chart; be able to understand and evaluate the contribution of others in the small group, and incorporate worthwhile ideas on one's own Case Preparation Chart; be able to contribute to group effectiveness and cohesion by concentrating on value adding ideas; manage group time effectively and maintain the morale of the group and its members. In this stage, each participant learns to work effectively in a small group or team, and has to be able to provide valuable inputs and incorporate useful ideas from others in his or her own perspective. The participant also has to learn to recognize what constitutes satisfactory group preparation for the next stage: large group discussion.

Stage 3 - Large Group Discussion

There are a number of learning objectives specific to the large group discussion. Clearly, many of the learning objectives for the Case Difficulty Cube and individual and small group work become reinforced in the large group. The participant must be able to contribute his or her ideas when called upon or volunteer at the appropriate time. The participant must be able to listen actively and assess the class discussion against his or her own Case Preparation Chart. The participant must be able to identify where other contributors present ideas that coincide or disagree with his or her own. The participant must be able to update his or her Case Preparation Chart. In the large group, the participant learns to work effectively with others and test his or her own individual and small group work against the large group result. Communication skills such as critical listening, effective speaking, evaluating others and learning to build on the ideas of others are also an integral part of large group discussion.

Learning Objectives and the Case Preparation Chart

The Case Preparation Chart gives an organizational context to a different set of learning objectives. During both the Short and Long Cycle Processes the participant is exposed to a successive set of steps which encourage learning as summarized in Exhibits 3-2 and 3-3.

The Long Cycle Process is the intellectual core of the case method, focusing on analytical and conceptual skills as well as the data management skills of the presentation dimension. The content of the Long Cycle Process is what most of the small group and large group case discussion time should be focused on.

Exhibit 3-2
LEARNING OBJECTIVES AND
THE SHORT CYCLE PROCESS

Step 2	Learning Objectives
Who/Position	Learn to identify with a specific position in an organization and to put oneself into another person's position.
What	Learn to identify with the types of decisions connected with a particular position in an organization and become acquainted with the range of responsibilities attached. Learn to become skilled with issue and problem identification.
Why	Learn to define causes and effects and the chronological sequence of events in a specific context.
When	Learn to develop a time plan, recognizing the time required to do certain tasks and specific time constraints.
How	Learn to assess a case on the analytical, conceptual and presentation dimensions of the Case Difficulty Cube.

Exhibit 3-3
LEARNING OBJECTIVES AND
THE LONG CYCLE PROCESS

Part 2	Learning Objectives
Immediate Issue(s)	Learn to recognize and focus on the immediate task(s) to be resolved. Learn to prioritize if more than one task needs to be addressed in a specific organizational context.
Basic Issue(s)	Be able to put the immediate issue into a larger context. Develop the ability to generalize. Take a particular decision beyond the case specifics into the course context and into the real-life large picture. See the connection between a variety of basic issues and their interplay in a specific real-life situation.
Importance/ Urgency Matrix	Be able to assess both the importance and the urgency of an issue in an organizational context. Be able to prioritize and provide a context for an eventual alternative selection and action and implementation plan.
Cause and Effect Diagram	Learn to identify and categorize the variety of causes contributing to a specific effect or outcome. This diagram is a key analytical tool for a host of management situations where improvement is sought.
Other Analytical Tools, Theories, Techniques	Learn to apply additional tools, theories and techniques which may be course specific or related to the decision making model in general. Learn how to distinguish the appropriateness of various theoretical perspectives to the decision or issue under consideration and how to apply concepts correctly. Learn both the usefulness and limitations of various theories, concepts and tools.
Alternative Generation	Develop creative skills to generate a list of potential alternatives.

Exhibit 3–3 (continued)

Part 2	Learning Objectives
Decision Criteria	Be able to identify qualitative and quantitative criteria tied to the context provided in the case and appropriate in view of the importance/urgency matrix assessment. Be able to prioritize both qualitative and quantitative decision criteria.
Assessment of Alternatives	Be able to assess quantitative versus qualitative trade-offs and connect alternatives to the importance/urgency matrix.
Selection of Preferred Alternative	Be able to make a decision. Be able to move from an analytical mode into a decision mode.
Prediction of Outcomes	Be able to look ahead to consequences flowing from decisions, forecasting and predicting quantitative and qualitative outcomes. Learn how to develop and evaluate best and worst outcome scenarios.
Action/ Implement-ation Plan	Be able to plan a series of actions which lead to a desired result. Be able to tie the financial, physical, human, and technological resources to a chronology with a specific deadline.
Missing Information	Learn to identify missing relevant information, assessing its potential availability, location, time and cost of collection, and impact of the missing information on the decision and plans at hand.
Assumptions	Learn to distinguish between facts and assumptions and develop a reasonable assumption. Learn to live in a world with incomplete information. Be able to assess the impact of assumptions made on decisions, actions and implementation plans and be able to develop alternative scenarios if an assumption is found to be incorrect.

Learning Objectives and
Skill Development Overview

In the introduction to *Learning with Cases* eight participant skills are listed as reasons for the use of the case method. These are analytical, decision making, application, oral communication, time management, interpersonal/social, creative and written communication skills.

It is possible to connect these skills to the Case Difficulty Cube, the Three Stage Learning Process and the Short and Long Cycle Processes culminating in the Case Preparation Chart. Exhibit 3-4 provides an overview where the maximum impact of skill development is likely to occur when viewed from these three different perspectives.

The Participant as a Starting Point

It is useful to identify the education, experience and cultural background of those who will be participating. It is quite different if the class participants have never used cases before, than if all participants have extensive case experience. Similarly, if the participant group has a single company affiliation, such as for an in-house program, it is quite different from a group with a varied organizational background, such as a public program. Maturity and work experience of the participants is always relevant and, particularly, with respect to the subject matter taught. Teaching a marketing course using cases to non-marketing people is quite different from teaching it to marketing professionals.

The educational background of participants is also relevant. What conceptual and theoretical building blocks are already in place at the start of the course? For case teaching, the participants' level of qualitative and quantitative skills will also be a factor in course design.

Exhibit 3-4

SKILL DEVELOPMENT, THE CASE DIFFICULTY CUBE,
THE THREE STAGE LEARNING PROCESS AND THE CASE PREPARATION CHART

Skill	Case Difficulty Cube			Three Stage Learning Process			Case Preparation Chart	
	A Axis	C Axis	P Axis	Individual	Small Group	Large Group	Short Cycle	Long Cycle
Analytical	✓			✓	✓	✓	✓	✓
Decision Making	✓	✓		✓	✓	✓		✓
Application		✓		✓	✓	✓		✓
Oral Communication					✓	✓		
Time Management		✓	✓	✓	✓		✓	✓
Interpersonal/Social		✓			✓	✓		
Creative	✓	✓	✓	✓	✓	✓		✓
Written Communication				✓			✓	✓

Constraints

Instructors have to design courses within the constraints of their teaching environment. For example, time allotted for the class, the number of classes, the amount of student preparation, the facilities, the budget and the attitudes towards case teaching within the institution will affect the options available.

The essential point in setting the learning objectives for a course revolves around the old adage, "If you don't know where you are going, any road will do." Certain roads will be cut off by time constraints, administrative policies, student level, student mix and other factors beyond the control of the instructor. Nonetheless, many roads will remain open and it is up to the instructor to specify the learning priorities and goals. The better this activity in course planning is executed, the more valuable it becomes for both instructors and students.

THE GENERAL COURSE DESIGN

Once the learning objectives have been established, it is possible to proceed with the general course design. The assumption that these two are sequential is probably naive. Most people seem to proceed with both simultaneously, adjusting each with every iteration. The end product of general course design is a topic sequence outline by major modules, along with the number of class and case sessions within each module. For example, Exhibit 3-5 gives a generalized course outline by headings.

New Course Design

New course design normally starts with an overview of the literature from which the instructor selects the topic areas most relevant for the course. If an instructor wishes

Exhibit 3-5
GENERALIZED COURSE OUTLINE

Course Title:

Target Student Group:

Educational Objectives:

Topic Outline	# of Sessions/ Classes	# of Cases
A. Introduction	3	1
B. Major Topic X Sub-topic 1 Sub-topic 2	7	4
C. Major Topic Y Sub-topic 1 Sub-topic 2 Sub-topic 3	7	3
D. Major Topic Z Sub-topic 1 Sub-topic 2	8	5
E. Conclusion/ Overview	2	1

to use cases in the course, discussion with leading practitioners in the field can provide valuable guidance, both to major topic areas and to potential cases.

Interviews with practitioners are helpful to identify the frequency and magnitude of typical decisions they face as part of their job responsibilities. These decisions should be reflected in the case choices made by the case course designer.

Course Redesign

For most instructors, new course design is something which occurs infrequently. The normal task is one of course redesign.

Course redesign may be major or minor depending on the maturity of the course. Since cases age, there is always a need to remove old cases and insert new ones as standard course maintenance. What percentage of cases should be replaced after completion of each course will depend on instructor and student preferences, the speed of change in the field and the availability of suitable new cases.

Student feedback on specific course segments, cases and inputs from colleagues teaching the same course are also valuable for course redesign.

When multiple instructors teach the same course, course redesign becomes a group process in which strong personal preference for inclusion of certain cases may have to be negotiated. There is always a trade-off between re-using an old case an instructor knows how to teach well and a new, but untried case. Thus, it is useful to have guidelines for case replacement, such as: every case in this course will be less than five years old and twenty percent of all cases will be replaced annually.

In addition to the positioning of segments within a course, the process of rationalization and sequencing between various courses in a program is often an issue in course design, especially in required courses. For example, some concepts and tools, such as relevant costs and discounted cash flows, normally should be presented before applications and analysis are introduced in other courses.

Even with the topic outline in place and the number of classes assigned per topic, it is not safe to assume the final course outline will adhere to the general design. Once detailed planning has started, new information may become available resulting in further modifications. Obviously, there is no easy answer to the selection of topics and the number of class sessions per topic. It appears to be a trial and error process which may well extend over a number of years. Continued questioning and vigilance is necessary to avoid the trap of complacency.

In the sequencing of major modules, prerequisite knowledge and skills form a theoretically logical basis. Where and when to use cases may be built on the same logic, but may also depend on what other instructors are doing in the program, the availability of suitable case material, the type of participant group and the instructor's personal preferences.

DETAILED PLANNING — SEQUENCING SESSIONS AND SELECTING MATERIALS

Detailed planning concerns itself with the sequence of individual sessions and the selection of materials. In teaching with cases, the instructor must be concerned about how to integrate theory and practice in making the appropriate sequencing decisions.

Integrating Theory and Practice in Course Design

One of the enduring academic questions in business education has been whether to integrate theory with practice. The strategy to remain totally at the theoretical, conceptual content or totally at the application end has been debated by the respective adherents. However, the debate in many ways is sterile and non-productive.

The issue should no longer be one of whether to integrate theory with practice but rather of how. Should students first get exposure through some cases to a few practical problems so that they can identify a need for a theory or derive a theory? Or should the theory be given first and then the practical problems for application? There are inherent advantages and disadvantages to each approach, consequently both may have to be used in a successful course design.

Material Selection

Material selection and sequencing are interdependent decisions. In material selection the emphasis in this text will be on the selection of cases, even though the existence of many other options is recognized. For example: lectures, reading discussions, business games, field trips, student presentations, videos, visitors to class, simulations, exercises, role plays, programmed instruction, and projects are just some of the options which may be used with or without cases.

Case options include a wide variety across the Case Difficulty Cube spectrum as well as sequential or series cases, illustrative cases, historical cases and incident cases. Not all of these options are appropriate for all courses nor should one attempt to include them all in any one course design. However, based on the learning objectives and the major conceptual modules as laid out earlier, some combination of these various methods is entirely appropriate and probably desirable. A selected short list of these methods will be discussed in Chapter 8. Only the two basic materials, cases and readings, will be covered in this chapter.

Case Selection

Instructors have a variety of decision criteria regarding what case to select for a particular slot of the course. Criteria include:

1. Fit with the course framework
2. Position on the Case Difficulty Cube
3. Teachability or instructor's comfort level with the case
4. Participant preference or interest
5. Length of case
6. Sequence of previous or subsequent cases
7. Age of case
8. Amount of qualitative or quantitative analysis required
9. Amount of time in class devoted to non-case materials or activities
10. Fit with other courses taught to same participant group in terms of topic and or timing
11. Position of key decision maker, industry, location or organizational setting
12. Recommendations of others
13. Any combination of the above

The more convinced the instructor is that a particular case fits a certain slot in the course, the easier it will be for the participants to come to the same conclusion. And the participant's perception of the worth of a particular case and its appeal are important motivators for engaging properly in the Three Stage Learning Process.

Participants' Favorite Cases

The selection of cases suitable for a particular course goes well beyond the standard issue, industry, company criteria. Participants know that some cases are memorable and others not. Given that participant motivation and excitement are important components in the overall learning process, paying attention to factors which participants consider important in assessing cases may help the overall acceptance of a course.

Qualities of cases which participants consider highly attractive can be tied into the Case Preparation Chart. A student's first reaction after the Short Cycle Process will significantly influence his or her energy level and excitement in preparing the case carefully.

Who. Participants are more interested if they can see themselves in the position of the decision maker shortly after they leave school or a reasonable time into the future. Likewise, if the organization itself is well known and respected and not disguised, it is also positive. Cases that are located in a geographical area of the world where the students expect to be working are also preferred.

What. If the immediate and basic issues are seen as relevant to the course and to the participants' future experiences, then student reaction is positive. A second dimension here deals with the size and excitement over the issue. A failure to balance the books by $100 is not nearly as interesting as a failure to balance the books by several million dollars. A third dimension deals with the product or service involved. A case about marketing a new computer game is more exciting than marketing a liver pill for 90-year-olds. Cases that tell a story, have an interesting plot and fleshed-out characters are also appealing.

Why. Cases that have clear causes or action triggers for creating the issue or opportunity are more interesting to students than those that have no apparent reason. A significant competitive move, an organizational crisis or a request from one's boss more readily capture participant involvement.

When. There are a number of issues surrounding the time and timing of the case. Generally speaking, the more recent the case the better. Cases set in time periods before participants were born may well fit the educational purpose beautifully, but they fail at the appreciation polls. Similarly, cases where there is a significant time pressure tend to be more exciting than those that require eventual resolution.

How. The Case Difficulty Cube position also impacts receptivity by students. Short cases tend to be preferred over longer cases and well organized cases tend to be preferred over cases poorly presented. A lot of extraneous information is disgusting. A lot of missing information makes it easy to give up. A lot of different formats may take too much time. Clearly, the (3, 3, 3) type of cases tend to be unpopular, unless enough time is provided to allow for proper preparation before class. On the other extreme, (1, 1, 1) types of cases can be perceived as trivial.

Each step in the Long Cycle Process will condition the continuing intensity of student involvement in case preparation.

The Importance/Urgency Matrix. Cases of importance to the organization are preferred. Urgency is somewhat less significant, particularly for important issues. Having appropriate time available in the case context to resolve an important issue properly is preferable over having to take shortcuts.

The Cause and Effect Diagram. Playing the commercial detective can be lots of fun provided sufficient clues are available in the case. Diagnosing what did not go according to plan and why is a fundamental role in management that students easily appreciate.

Alternative Generation. Better cases have significantly different and opposed alternatives. Innovative alternatives are preferable over standard suggestions.

Decision Criteria. Cases with both quantitative and qualitative criteria requiring careful prioritization beat those that just need to meet a financial target.

Alternative Assessment. Cases that require a decision, scary as it may be for some students, tend to be better than "talk about, don't decide" types of cases. Cases containing alternatives which can make a significant difference in the future tend to be preferable.

Action/Implementation Plan. Cases which contain sufficient information to put a realistic plan forward tend to be better.

Missing Information. Cases where not too much critical information is missing tend to be preferable.

Assumptions. Cases which permit participants to make realistic assumptions are preferable as are those which require little guessing as to what might be reasonable.

Samples, videos, and visitors to class add reality and importance and relevance. It should also be noted that an exciting instructor can make a big difference in the reception of a case.

Not every class will react the same way to every case. Timing in the course or program, factors in the environment that affect preparation or the mood of the class may quickly alter perceptions. Changes in assignment questions and the way the class is taught can have a huge impact. Many participants who have experienced cases in their educational background can recall years later some of the outstanding case experiences they have had, quoting case and, occasionally, the instructor by name.

That certain cases are more memorable than others is no secret. Putting a course together with only memorable cases is probably not possible. Trying to include cases which fit educational objectives as well as impress participants is an integral part of effective material selection.

Case Selection and the Case Difficulty Cube

The Case Difficulty Cube may provide a rationale for case sequencing and selection within a course. For instructors who wish to intimidate their students at the beginning of the course, a (3, 3, 3) type of case, well beyond the capability of the class, may give an introduction to the course which says, "Right now you cannot handle this, but by the end of the course you will be able to." Thus, the same case can serve as an introduction and conclusion to the course and participants can assess their own progress. Other instructors believe that the case challenge and difficulty has to match the capability of the participants. They might start a course with a (2, 1, 1) case and gradually increase the difficulty level across the three dimensions. Thus, for the cases chosen a potential sequence might be as shown in Exhibit 3-6.

Exhibit 3-6
A COURSE OUTLINE RANKING CASES BY
THEIR CASE DIFFICULTY CUBE POSITION

Class	Case	Class	Case
1	2, 1, 1	8	2, 3, 2
2	2, 2, 1	9	3, 1, 1
3	2, 1, 2	10	3, 2, 1
4	1, 2, 2	11	3, 3, 1
5	2, 2, 2	12	3, 3, 2
6	1, 3, 1	13	3, 3, 3
7	2, 3, 1		

Depending on the instructor's objectives, there are many potential combinations. Certain patterns may be repeated at various times of the course for review and reinforcement. A total measure of difficulty may be established by using the arithmetic sum of the three dimensions. A total of 3 to 6, for example, ranges from easy at 3 to medium at 6. From 7 to 9, the case would be on the upper end of the scale with a (3, 3, 3) case being clearly very difficult.

Additional Reading/Data Gathering

Additional reading and data gathering in a course which uses cases need to be selected and planned with the same care as the cases and other materials. Since most instructors are familiar with the selection and specification of reading materials, the few comments here are directly related to the connection with cases.

Course readings are often specifically relevant in terms of the theoretical objectives of the course. Sometimes it is possible to assign specific readings which fit perfectly with the immediate and/or basic issues in the case. A good example would be a case where the key issue deals with the application of the learning curve to a pricing or scheduling issue and the reading covers the theoretical aspects of the learning curve or manufacturing progress function. Such a perfect fit is not always possible, however, and additional readings may be useful from a course, but not a specific case perspective. Whenever readings are assigned along with cases, the amount of reading time needs to be added to the expected case preparation time. There is always a concern that if the total time required exceeds the participants' willingness or ability to devote to it, then the trade-offs — skip the reading or skip the case preparation — become counter-productive. Separating readings into required and optional may be one way of distinguishing the relevance and importance of readings from the instructor's perspective.

Cases which require additional data gathering from the Internet or other sources permit a learning dimension generally not available with most standard cases. To be able to do original research or data gathering is in itself a worthwhile educational objective. The same caution regarding participant time applies, however.

DEFINING THE PERFORMANCE EVALUATION MEASURES

The fourth common element in course planning deals with defining the performance evaluation measures. If cases are used in the course, what weight will case work carry as part of the overall course grade and how will case performance be measured? In this chapter we will discuss the definition of performance measures related to the use of cases. In Chapters 6 and 7 the way instructors go about evaluating case performance and how they provide feedback will be the key topics. In Chapter 5 of *Learning with Cases* effective and ineffective participation are discussed and a number of examples for participants to consider are provided.

Every course plan and syllabus needs to indicate how participants will be graded, whether cases are used or not. On the assumption that at least some recognition will be given to case work, the first question deals with the percentage of total course grade devoted to cases. The most common case activities which are assigned grades are class participation, case presentation, case reports and case exams.

Weighting Schemes

It is not surprising that considerable variation exists on the course weights assigned to case related work. Generally, the fewer cases used in the course, the lower the weighting of case related work should be. Some instructors feel strongly that every course component needs to have a grade attached to it to motivate participants to do the work. Other instructors are of the opinion that such a strong grading focus stands in the way of effective learning. They argue that, provided the instructor can explain the educational value of various course components, grading should be downplayed. Both camps have ardent followers who can prove their point with personal experiences. Thus, it appears that strength of conviction as to which path is right is a greater factor in successful application than either path itself.

It does seem reasonable that in a course composed a hundred percent of cases, the course grade should be based on case work. Even here, how much of the course grade should be based on class participation as opposed to the final case exam still needs to be resolved. Given that courses can have a case use ratio between 0 and 100%, it is reasonable to have a variety of weightings, partially based on the course objectives, case frequency in the course, and the role cases play in the course.

The second aspect of case grade weighting concerns the division between class participation and written work. Class participation includes the normal large group or class discussion as well as presentations. Written work includes hand-ins, case reports and case exams.

One reasonable rule for allocating course grades for various case related components is to estimate the total participant time required for each component and assign grade portions accordingly. Notice that strict adherence to such a rule would lower the final exam (if a case) impact significantly compared to regular class participation (see Chapter 6.)

THE FIRST FEW CLASSES

In any course using a reasonable number of cases with participants who have little or no case experience, it is important to design the first few classes to introduce both the course and the case method. One effective way is to use a small, one-page case in the very first class, hand it out at the beginning of the class and go through the Three Stage Learning Process right in class. It is useful for the instructor to explain some of the key points regarding each stage before having the participants do each stage. For example, the instructor can reinforce the importance of taking ownership of the position of the decision maker in the case before the participants do individual preparation. Small group guidelines can be explained before the small group discussions start. Common understandings on large group discussion can be reviewed before the third stage. In addition the first class may deal with: (1) introductions, seating arrangements, name cards, personal background sheets, the class photo; (2) the course plan, the number of cases and why they will be used, when and how; and (3) the assignments for the next few classes in detail.

Some instructors prefer to leave the course syllabus to the second or a later class, focusing primarily on establishing class norms regarding case use and discussion in the first few classes. The key course planning decision for the first few classes is how much course and class time to devote to the case learning process versus the course content. Some instructors make comments like, "For as far as course content goes, I see the first few classes as throw-aways." Others still manage to hold on to some course content by using the early classes to teach some basic simple building blocks, while simultaneously covering the participative aspects of the learning process.

Given the importance of starting off on the right foot, it is certainly appropriate to plan opening classes carefully. Class participants will very quickly perceive norms like: Is the instructor fair? Does the instructor appear to know what he or she is doing? Is everyone expected to participate? What kind of comment is acceptable or unacceptable?

In our experience, the text *Learning with Cases* can be a valuable aid for participants to get up to speed quickly on the use of cases. In a three class module it is possible to introduce the Three Stage Learning Process and Case Difficulty Cube in the first class, the Short and Long Cycle Processes and Case Preparation Chart in the second class and class participation in the third class, along with a one-page case in the first class, a three-page case in the second, and a five to six-page case in the third class.

COMMUNICATING THE COURSE PLAN

Most instructors believe that a detailed course outline is necessary to help students understand the particular area of study and its scope.

Normally, a course outline contains sections regarding:

- Target audience
- What the course is trying to achieve
- How it will be taught
- How performance will be measured
- Standards for satisfactory performance
- How final grades will be determined
- The course plan by major modules and session sequence
- Case and other assignments

In courses using cases, the course plan should indicate why cases are included in the course and how students are expected to prepare for and participate in the Three Stage Learning Process.

Instructors often assign the course syllabus as reading for the first, second or third class in the course and allocate class time for an appropriate discussion of its key elements.

CONCLUSION

The course planning process is a difficult one for many. Most instructors would like to be able to accomplish more than they realize they can, so that what not to include is as much a decision as what to include. There are no easy solutions available and the course design task appears to be iterative through objectives, general and detailed planning, to material selection and back again. Trade-offs are inevitable in this kind of process and once teaching groups get involved, negotiation may have to be used to reach a common agreement. For many, a written document, the course plan or syllabus, is the final product of this process which normally, but not always, is distributed to students.

preparation for class

Proper preparation, both by instructors and participants, is required to make case teaching and learning effective.

In terms of basic minimum requirements, such as becoming thoroughly familiar with the case content, analyzing and making judgments regarding case information, participants and instructors have a common individual preparation task. Beyond this common level their respective tasks change. Students in some schools often have two or three such preparations per day, four or five days per week. Teachers seldom face such a large number of preparations. However, instructors must go well beyond the student level of preparation for the case and must prepare strategies and plans for conducting the class.

The student preparation task has been well covered in Chapter 3 of *Learning with Cases*. Instructors will find this information not only applicable as a key part of their own preparation, but also helpful in counseling students, since students need coaching in order to develop case analysis skills.

This chapter will begin with the standard why, when and how long questions for instructor preparation. It will then shift to the content, priority and execution aspects of preparation, followed by the teaching note. The chapter will next cover the Case Teaching Plan, a comprehensive tool to guide instructors in the classroom, and conclude with teaching files and teaching meetings.

WHY PREPARE?

Proper preparation by participants as well as their instructor is vital to effective case learning and teaching. Moreover, the evidence of sound teacher preparation in class sets a powerful example for participants to commit themselves to equal diligence in their own preparation.

WHEN TO PREPARE?

The instructor's preparation is a continuation of a process that started with course planning wherein case selection and sequence were established. The time span has now shortened and the instructor must prepare for the class scheduled in the course plan.

Some instructors prefer to leave this preparation to the day before the actual class is taught or even the same day to keep case facts clear in their mind. Others think more lead time is necessary to account for emergencies and to provide more time to reflect on case content and the teaching process.

When instructors prepare several days in advance of the actual class, they normally review their preparation for 15-30 minutes on the actual day of teaching to refresh their memory.

HOW LONG DOES IT TAKE TO PREPARE?

The instructor new to case teaching is sometimes surprised to learn of the extensive time required for a case class preparation. A simple rule of thumb for the experienced instructor is that it takes at least three times as long to prepare as the class length, provided he or she has taught this case before. A new instructor may significantly exceed this preparation time. Of course, time required to prepare will also depend on the length and complexity of the case and whether a teaching note already exists or needs to be developed.

HOW TO PREPARE

The instructor's preparation may be divided into three major categories: content, priority, and execution.

The Content Focus

Instructor preparation starts at the same point as student preparation and continues with more rigor through exactly the same steps outlined in the approach for individual preparation by participants in Chapter 3 of *Learning with Cases*. Just like students, instructors need to go through the Short and Long Cycle Processes of case preparation and prepare a Case Preparation Chart. Different from students who need to know where the information can be found in the case, instructors must be thoroughly familiar with the key case facts. Knowing the case facts and doing a complete analysis of the information are basic for content-focused preparation.

The Priority Focus

Preparatory activities also have a priority focus. These activities include a review of course objectives, case objectives, and plans for this particular class within the sequence of all classes. Why is it so important to have this class and this case within this class? The implication of priority planning is that, given time in class as a scarce resource, priority topics will receive preference over others. In teaching with cases, priorities may lie with making sure that certain concepts are fully understood, an objective that parallels many other forms of teaching. Particular to cases may be the priorities dealing with problem identification and analysis, alternative generation, decision making, implementation planning, sorting or specification of information and proper application of relevant theory to practice.

In the first few classes in a case course, priority may well lie with getting the class familiar with the discussion process and the instructor's expectations regarding proper student preparation and participation in class. Priorities in case teaching are, therefore, multi-dimensional, and are both process and content based.

The Execution Focus

The execution focus relates to how the class will be conducted. The instructor has to address the following questions. What would I like to happen in class? How can I make it happen? Who should contribute in class? What is the best order for the discussion, decision first and then analysis? Vice versa? How much time is necessary for discussion of the various case components? Should I leave the class unstructured? What teaching aids are available that I could bring to class? The responses to questions of this type are vital to effective instructor preparation.

The content and priority preparation work is reflected during the execution in a student assignment, a time plan, a board plan and a participation plan. Even though a theoretical argument can be advanced for treating content, priority and execution as three distinct chronological phases of instructor preparation, in reality these are normally intertwined.

TEACHING OR INSTRUCTOR NOTES

Teaching or instructor notes are materials intended to be helpful for anyone teaching the case. Teaching notes should only be available to instructors and must be kept from student hands or eyes. The content-focused parts of the teaching note should initially be prepared by the case author during the writing stage as a quality control check on data completeness and clarity. However, it is sound practice for anyone teaching a case for the first time to create his or her own teaching note during the instructor preparation phase. Then, this note can be compared to the existing teaching note, if one is available.

Teaching or instructor notes come from different sources. Teaching notes normally accompany published case textbooks. Publishers would have difficulty selling case texts without them! Other sources include case clearing centers, colleagues and one's own files.

The quality of teaching notes will vary considerably from author to author. Since a teaching note has been written within the context of a particular course, each instructor has to ask whether these same conditions pertain to the course under consideration. A straight transplant of a case to another environment or another course may not produce the desired results. The instructor must ask , "Can I find a way to make this case work for me?" In the end, every instructor must develop his or her own teaching note.

Normal teaching note topics include: identification of the educational objectives and the case issues, a suggested student assignment, questions which could be asked during the class discussion, and comments regarding the analysis and solution. There is no standard format for teaching notes although many of the potential teaching note headings in Exhibit 4-1 are included in most teaching notes.

Exhibit 4-1
POTENTIAL TEACHING NOTE HEADINGS

1. Case Title

2. Brief Synopsis of the Case

3. Teaching Objectives

4. Immediate Issue(s) *(the case decision maker's key concerns)*

5. Basic Issue(s) *(the instructor's reasons for using the case in the course)*

6. Suggested Additional Reading

7. Possible Teaching Aids *(such as samples, advertising material, photos, articles, videos, computer programs, CD ROMs, visitors to class)*

8. Suggested Student Assignment

9. Potential Discussion Questions for Use in Class *(to use if the discussion dies or a change of direction is desirable)*

10. Case Analysis *(the responses to the suggested student assignment questions, including the Case Preparation Chart)*

11. Additional Points to Raise *(beyond the student assignment questions; may include what actually happened)*

12. Teaching Suggestions

13. Case Teaching Plan *(the instructor's agenda, time, participation and board plans for the class)*

The following comments cover each of the headings identified in Exhibit 4-1.

1. *Title.* It is normal to give the case title and either above or below the case title add Teaching Note or Instructor's Note as a second title.

2. *Brief Synopsis of the Case.* Many teaching notes provide a brief synopsis of the case which may be a one or two paragraph summary of the case or the opening paragraph.

3. *Teaching Objectives.* The teaching objectives for the case normally identify the course in which the case is used and where in this course the case fits as well as the type of student expected to take the course. Teaching objectives can be identified along the three dimensions of the Case Difficulty Cube as shown in Exhibit 4-2.

Exhibit 4-2
THE BRIEF STATEMENT OF TEACHING OBJECTIVES

Analytical Dimension

The student should be able to develop the following skills:
- Identify a problem/issue/decision or opportunity
- Evaluate a decision already taken
- Analyze a problem or issue
- Develop decision criteria
- Develop and evaluate alternatives
- Generate an action and implementation plan

Conceptual Dimension

The student should be able to understand and apply the following:
- Theory(ies)
- Concept(s)
- Technique(s)

Presentation Dimension

The student should be able to:
- Separate relevant from available information
- Specify relevant missing information
- Organize information logically
- Develop appropriate assumptions
- Practice data retrieval

4. *Immediate Issues.* Immediate issues are decisions, problems, concerns, challenges, opportunities or issues facing the focal decision maker in the case.

5. *Basic Issues.* Basic issues are those that made the instructor select the case for inclusion in the course design. Basic issues are usually expressed as topics in the course outline and in the theoretical readings assigned along with the case.

6. *Suggested Additional Readings.* It is normal to assign additional readings from a textbook, articles or other sources along with the case. These readings may pertain directly to the accompanying case or be assigned in advance of future classes or to complement prior classes.

7. *Possible Teaching Aids.* Teaching Aids may include samples, photographs, newspaper and magazine clippings, articles, web pages, annual reports, ads or videos that can help augment the reality of a case and stimulate class discussion.

   Samples of company products can be brought to class and passed around. They are a simple but effective way of reinforcing the reality of the case. Similarly, if samples are not possible to obtain, photographs may help. If the instructor brings, or encourages students to bring, newspaper and magazine clippings to class, these can be put on a notice board and may provide new information on problems and organizations discussed in class. These aids and others, such as articles, annual reports and company ads, are not usually the types of things that make or break the case, but they show that the instructor cares and wants to make the class as interesting and relevant as possible.

Films and videos can be used to present information traditionally committed to paper. Aside from their visual appeal, they may offer a more realistic understanding of the company situation. In addition, videos can easily be made when special visitors are invited to class. These videos can be shown in subsequent classes and generate further insights into the case as well as substantial interest among participants.

8. *Suggested Student Assignment.* The student assignment identifies specific questions related to the case. Additional readings may also be called for in the same assignment. When such assignments are communicated to students and what form they take vary in practice. Assignments may be handed out as part of a course outline, posted on the Internet or announced at the start of the preceding class.

Usually, assignments are provided at the beginning of the course or at intervals during the term. When the assignment is given during class it is likely to be brief.

Usually, one case is assigned to one class.

Sometimes if the case falls in the (3, 3, 3) level of difficulty, it may be assigned over two or three class periods. Occasionally, the assignment for the next class is given in the preceding class.

Student assignments will reflect the learning goals and expectations of the instructor. Assignment questions should be consistent with the course objectives and customized for each class.

The three standard assignment questions which can be asked for almost all cases are:

1. If you were in the position of... (the decision maker) in the... case, what would be your analysis of... (the decision, problem, issue, challenge or opportunity)?

2. What decision would you take and why?

3. What would be your action/implementation plan?

The kind of assignment given with a case can significantly influence the student's preparation and the subsequent class discussion. Take, for example, a case describing a merger proposal. The following two different sets of assignment questions could substantially change the use of this case.

A. If you were the president of the initiating company:

1. What would be your major proposal?

2. What would be your prediction of the potential future market share and sales volume for the merged company?

Compare these two questions to the following:

B. If you were the president of the target company:

1. What would be your conditions for a merger proposal to be acceptable?

2. What major obstacles would you expect to encounter if a merger were to be proposed?

Variation in case assignments allows the same case to be used for a variety of purposes and courses. Whereas, because of copyright restrictions, instructors cannot change any part of any case, unless they authored the case, no such restrictions exist on student assignment questions. Therefore, it is perfectly reasonable for an instructor to change the student orientation to the case by including certain provisions within the assignment questions. Examples include:

1. If this case took place currently instead of ten years ago, how would your analysis change?

2. If this case took place in our country ....

3. If this company were profitable ...

4. If this company were not profitable ....

5. If this were a public organization ....

If the assignment question requires too much preparation time of the participant, there are some simple ways to decrease this time. For example, it is possible to minimize calculation time by providing a spreadsheet or partial analysis where most calculations have already been completed and only a few remain.

Some instructors believe that highly detailed case assignments are necessary, while others prefer more general questions. If the participant audience is thoroughly familiar with the case method, no assignment questions may be necessary. It is possible to start with detailed case questions at the beginning of a course and gradually change to more general questions as the course progresses.

9. *Potential Discussion Questions for Use in Class.* Potential questions the instructor may wish to ask in class are different from the assignment questions. They are intended to be stimulants for further discussion should the class discussion lag or veer off topic, but different from the generic questions any instructor can ask with any case.

In the teaching note these additional questions are, therefore, case specific and might have been included in the assigned student questions, if the assignment had been more extensive. (The discussion of potential case specific questions which fit the analytical, conceptual and presentation dimensions of the case is provided in Chapter 5.) For the merger example discussed above, sample additional questions could be: What could be the key characteristics of another merger prospect for this company? Is it possible to perform a SWOT (Strengths, Weaknesses, Opportunities and Threats) analysis on both of these companies?

10. *Case Analysis.* The case analysis and Case Preparation Chart section of the teaching note provides the answers to the questions assigned to the course participants. It is normally the most extensive part of any instructor's note and may be seen as a model written analysis if the case were to be used for a report or exam.

In the case analysis part of teacher preparation the course framework and supporting body of knowledge of the specific field are fundamental. Each instructor in each course is responsible for specifying the relevant theories and concepts with which students should be familiar by the end of the course. It is to reinforce the need for and application of these concepts and techniques that cases are used as part of the overall course design. Thus, in a financial course the type of analysis expected as part of proper case preparation will be totally different from the analysis expected in a marketing or human resources course. The analytical framework provided in the *Learning with Cases* text and this one focuses on the standard problem solving or decision making model which can be universally applied, provided it is properly integrated with the course specific theories and concepts.

The Case Preparation Chart discussed in Chapter 3 *Learning with Cases,* by itself, does not provide sufficient space to perform all of the analysis required, but serves as a useful summary of the analytical work done. Instructors should make a habit of filling out their own Case Preparation Chart for every case.

11. *Additional Points to Raise.* Additional points to raise form a section of the teaching note which allows the instructor to broaden the class discussion. For example, the instructor may wish to compare and or contrast one case with others taught in the same course or other courses or a current major issue reported in the media. Different from potential discussion questions, additional points will usually not be discussed extensively in class, and may be left with students to ponder after class.

12. *Teaching Suggestions.* Teaching suggestions comprise any advice someone who has taught the case may wish to share. Suggestions may be: remind the students during the previous class to do the calculations in units per hour; ask for a vote at the beginning, middle or end of the class; ask for volunteers; or stay away from a discussion of a specific issue or challenge.

   Teaching suggestions are case specific and accumulate as more experience is gained with the case. They may deal with any aspect of the Case Teaching Plan.

13. *The Case Teaching Plan.* The Case Teaching Plan in Exhibit 4-3 provides a valuable one page summary of the instructor's preparation for a specific class in which a case will be taught. Similar to the Case Preparation

Exhibit 4-3
CASE TEACHING PLAN

Case _____ Course _____ Date_____

Time
Plan   Agenda   **Participation Plan**

	Volunteer Preferences	

____ 1. Introduction

	5.
1.	5.
2.	6.
3.	7.
4.	8.

____ 2. Next/Other Classes

____ 3. Comments, Questions

                                          Volunteer (V)   **Call List**

____ 4. Reading Discussion   V or _____

____ 5. Case Introduction   V or _____

____ 6. Teaching Aids

____ 7. Assignment Questions

          If you were in the position of:

____   1_____   V or _____

____   2_____   V or _____

____   3_____   V or _____

____   4_____   V or _____

____ 8. Conclusion

____ Total

Board Plan

Issues	Analysis	Decision Criteria
		Action/Implementation
Analysis	Alternatives	Missing Info/Assumptions

Reference: *Teaching with Cases*, 2003, page 82

Chart for students, it provides the road map for the class for the instructor. It is not a substitute for the teaching note, but an integral part of it and the final step in instructor preparation. It indicates the what, when, who, and how of the coming class.

THE CASE TEACHING PLAN

The Case Teaching Plan has four parts: (1) agenda, (2) time plan, (3) participation plan and (4) board plan.

Agenda

Agenda items are potential topic areas or activities on which time could be spent during the class. Some instructors put this agenda, but seldom the time allocated to it, on the extreme left or right hand side of the board before class. Not all agenda items listed below need to occur in every class.

1. *Introduction* covers the first few minutes of a class usually well before the case discussion begins. On the assumption that a good start is half the battle, most instructors carefully prepare the beginning of every class.

   A simple way to start the class after the traditional good morning, afternoon or evening, is to note the agenda for the class including the case assignment questions. That way, the class can follow the sequence the instructor intends to follow. It is possible, but not necessary, to share the time plan as well as the agenda. Some instructors prefer to start with a cartoon or joke which, hopefully, has relevance to the key points of the class session. Some instructors start with administrative items.

2. *Next/Other Classes* is often used to provide the assignment(s) for the next class(es) and any special reminders the instructor may wish to give. Other classes refers to future classes beyond the next one or classes already completed, or some material or issues carried over from the last class. This section provides the instructor with the opportunity to place this class in the context of the course, and the course in the context of the program.

   If the instructor left the previous class unfinished or with one or more questions to review, this section of the class would usually cover such matters.

3. *Comments, Questions* may provide an opportunity for participants and the instructor to bring up news items that may be relevant to previous classes, the current one or future ones; or matters pertaining to the course or a specific class. This section may also give an opportunity for participants to bring up any non-course specific topics which they believe relevant and timely for the class or the program.

4. *Reading Discussion* deals with the additional readings assigned for the class. The instructor may invite questions from participants, or may ask questions, or provide a lecture to reinforce key points.

5. *Case Introduction* relates to the period just before discussion of the case starts. It provides an opportunity for the instructor to place the case in an industry or personal perspective. Questions like, "Has anyone worked in this industry or organization or faced this kind of decision?" are part of this phase. The case introduction can be seen as an opportunity to put the case in the context of the course or program and integrate it with topics covered by other instructors in other courses.

We do not advise a case introduction which includes a summary of the case to be discussed. If participants are properly prepared, such an introduction adds no value and consumes precious time. If participants are not properly prepared, the instructor should not send a message that poor preparation will be tolerated and compensated for by a lenient instructor.

6. *Teaching Aids.* If teaching aids are available for the case they are usually shown or passed around class before the actual case discussion begins.

7. *Assignment Questions* are the same ones given in the student assignment before class. If the questions are lengthy, they may be abbreviated on the Case Teaching Plan.

   There is a key underlying assumption in including the assignment questions and allocating time to each on the Case Teaching Plan. The instructor has gone to the trouble of carefully preparing assignment questions and communicating these to participants so that they can prepare their responses. Therefore, it is only appropriate that these questions and their answers be discussed in class. This does not mean that case discussion time needs to be focused solely on these questions. Experience shows that instructor failure to discuss assignment questions in class leads to students' ignoring the questions.

8. *Conclusion* refers to the ending of the class envisaged by the instructor. It reflects the priorities of the instructor. If only three concluding points can be made, what should they be and in what order? Will the instructor summarize, talk about what happened with respect to the decision or refer to the next class coming?

The conclusion to a case class, like the start, is a transition phase. Some instructors like it if students summarize the case discussion, although most feel this is a difficult role to ask a student to perform. Other instructors like to summarize the case and its key points themselves, perhaps commenting also on strengths and weaknesses evident in the class discussion of the case. Those who strongly believe in non-directive behavior prefer to leave the responsibility for evaluation of what happened in class and why on the shoulders of the participants and do not summarize or comment. The next chapter will present various ways of ending class. Some types of closure, such as summarizing the key points and lessons derived from the case, generalizing, or lecturing about the case will call for detailed preparation. Many instructors will have transparencies, handouts or digital projection material ready ahead of time for this purpose.

Other forms of closure will be more spontaneous, depending on what happened or did not happen in the classroom. Typical, for example, is when instructors wish to finish class with some kind of performance feedback. Obviously, the exact comments cannot be determined ahead of time, although it is wise to allow time for that type of closure.

Time Plan

The Time Plan shows the instructor's best guess regarding the length of time it will take to complete the various agenda items selected for a particular case class. Given that time is always scarce in a case discussion, it is generally a good idea to attempt to minimize the number of agenda items and maximize the amount of time allocated to case discussion.

The Time Plan refers to the anticipated time in minutes that may be spent on the various class agenda items. The total time cannot exceed the class time available. It is reasonable to indicate time estimates for each agenda item as a range, such as 5-8 minutes.

Participation Plan

The right hand side of the Case Teaching Plan relates to who will be expected to talk in class and when. It includes the students on the call list, volunteers and volunteer preferences.

The *Call List* is used to identify specific participants whom the instructor wishes to call on at various points during the class discussion. The main purposes of the call list are the following:

- To make sure everyone in the class participates at some point during the course.
- To identify students with particular skills and experiences that are relevant to a specific case situation.
- To ensure that, with a particularly difficult case, the right person starts.
- To establish class norms. For example, "It's not a good idea to come to my class without being prepared. I'll call on you!"
- To check student skills development. For example, "I want to check how well John opens a class. I need a reading on how well Angela is prepared." Or, "I wonder what kind of a job Maiko can do to summarize the discussion at the end of the class."
- To have a name available when no one volunteers in response to a question.

- To ensure that every person in class, whether the silent type or not, is called on.
- To force quiet students to speak in class.

There is no agreement as to whether instructors should use a call list. Those who choose to use them capitalize on some or all of the above purposes. Those who choose not to use them rely on and encourage voluntary class participation.

On the Case Teaching Plan the opportunities to call on participants occur in (4) reading discussion, (5) case introduction and (7) assignment questions or the case discussion. If a call list is used, the names of the people on the call list are written beside the agenda item. These names will not repeat on the volunteer preferences. As many as three or four participants can be listed on the call list for any agenda item in the sequence they will be called.

Volunteers. By circling the V for a particular agenda item the instructor indicates that he or she will ask for volunteers to discuss that particular agenda item. Generally, case courses taught solely by using volunteers tend to be dominated by a vocal minority in the class with a large group of non-participators as listeners. Therefore, call lists provide an alternative to inviting participation. If more than one person volunteers, the preference list is used to determine which participant will get the chance to speak.

Volunteer Preferences identifies those participants the instructor will call on when a choice among volunteers occurs. That is, when a number of participants indicate they wish to contribute simultaneously, the ones listed will be given priority. Volunteer Preferences may contain participants who seldom speak. This preparation makes it easier for the instructor during class when he or she has to choose among multiple volunteers.

The call list and the volunteer preferences are important tools for instructors who assign a grade for class participation or who wish to ensure that all members for the class participate actively throughout the course.

Board Plan

Many instructors like to plan ahead what they will record on the board. The location of certain comments may be predetermined, such as analysis on the left and recommendations on the right. Some teachers will even predetermine the color of chalk or marker which will be used.

The bottom of the Case Teaching Plan is reserved for the board plan. Those instructors who like to visualize what the end-result of the discussion recording task will be can use this as their miniaturized overview of the major discussion areas. The shadow headings on Exhibit 4-3 are suggestions only.

All of the blank space on the Case Teaching Plan provides the instructor with the opportunity to fill in comments specific to this class and case. The Case Teaching Plan in Exhibit 4-3, when magnified on a photocopier at a setting of 155%, becomes a letter size sheet which can be used for every class. It gives an early overview of the class which becomes a part of the teaching note/file for the next time the case is taught. Whereas most of the teaching note is likely to remain the same, the Case Teaching Plan details will change every time the case is taught.

The priority focus the instructor wishes to give to a particular case will be evident from the student assignment, the timing and board space allocations during class and the key points the instructor may wish to raise at the end of the class.

Our experience has been that the Case Teaching Plan is a valuable aid to effective case preparation as well as for the class session itself.

Appendix 3 contains an example of a small case with its teaching note, Case Preparation Chart and Case Teaching Plan.

TEACHING FILE

Instructors who teach the same case more than once typically have a teaching file, rather than just a teaching note. Every time he or she teaches the case, the teaching file grows with additional reflections on the Case Preparation Chart and Case Teaching Plans. It is also standard practice to include in the teaching file newspaper clippings, relevant readings and articles and web site information as they become available.

When several instructors teach the same case and course, it is good practice to share teaching notes and files and to have teaching meetings to discuss the teaching notes.

TEACHING MEETINGS

Just as small group discussion is a valuable part of the students' preparation task, many instructors find it helpful to talk over their case analyses and class plans with colleagues. Teaching group meetings are particularly helpful in courses having multiple sections and faculty and where consistency is expected.

A simple way to share the preparation for such teaching meetings is to have each faculty member volunteer to prepare and share ahead of time a teaching note and Case Teaching Plan (minus the participation plan) for a different case. Then, one teaching meeting may cover one or two cases coming up in the schedule and every faculty member is expected to come fully prepared for this meeting, even though one person has taken the lead.

CONCLUSION

Some teachers worry that an exhaustive preparation can only lead to a very directive and structured teaching approach. This is not true. Quite the opposite, flexibility is enhanced by preparation. Sound preparation is the ultimate prerequisite for effective case teaching and learning.

The time has now come to go to class. The course has been planned, cases selected, the participants have their assignment prepared, and the instructor has concluded his or her preparation. The true test of all this preparation is about to start.

CHAPTER FIVE

classroom process

The ultimate action place for teaching with cases is the classroom. This is where the results of planning and preparation will show. Since what happens in the classroom is by no means a standard process or procedure, it is useful to reinforce process variability at the start. Variation may depend on the objectives of the class, the subject matter, the type of case, the place in the sequence of classes, discussions in previous classes, or other classes in other courses taken simultaneously by the same participants. In addition, variation between classes will depend on the experience, teaching style and mood of the instructor, the qualifications and mood of the participants, the time of year, the weather, the political and economic news and, surely, other factors a teacher may be able to identify or guess at under the circumstances. That there is no such a thing as a standard case class which can be used as an objective model is unfortunate for those who seek imitation, and delightful for innovative teachers.

Even though a standard case class does not exist, we will create one, because many case classes do have some phases in common. From a discussion standpoint it is useful to have a reference base from which variations can be contrasted. Thus, this chapter will start with the description of such a reference class, followed by a discussion of its major phases in chronological order. Next will be a detailed discussion of the participative process with emphasis on questioning, responding, recording and dealing with participation problems. Finally, since a significant variant between instructors is the style employed by each, a discussion of case teaching styles will conclude the chapter.

THE REFERENCE CLASS

The following description of an actual class will be used as a reference for further detailed discussion. It is not meant to be an ideal model but does illustrate the use of the Case Preparation Chart and the Case Teaching Plan.

Professor Robert Jones walks into his class about five minutes before the 10:00 a.m. starting time. He checks to see if the board needs cleaning, if the projection equipment works, and exchanges a few pleasantries with the participants already in the class.

Next, on the far left side of the board he lists the agenda items from his Case Teaching Plan:

1. Introduction

2. Next Class

3. Field Trip

4. Reading

5. Case Title

If you were in the position of: .....
- Q1   What would be your analysis?
- Q2   What would be your alternatives and which one would you select and why?
6. Conclusion

He then removes a newspaper article from the notice board on the side wall (it refers to some current happenings in an industry discussed during a previous class) and positions himself near the center of the class to start promptly at ten o'clock.

"Good morning," he starts off and most of the class responds good-naturedly. "I am happy to see that you won the soccer game last Saturday, I'm expecting equally superior performance on the management field in this class today. Before we start the case discussion itself, let us settle a few things first." Professor Jones then discusses the agenda items he had written on the board and indicates that he expects volunteers for the first case question and names three specific individuals from different locations in the class to address the second case question and indicates in what sequence they will speak.

Next, he explains where the material for some future classes can be obtained and what special arrangements have been made for the coming field trip. He also explains how in this class he wishes to make sure that everybody understands the readings assigned along with the case, and that he wishes to start the class off with any issues arising from these readings. At this point, about five minutes have passed in the class.

The next ten minutes are devoted to a discussion of the readings. One student wants an explanation of a particular point on page 542 and the professor asks if anyone in the class can answer it. Three volunteer and the professor chooses one, who gives a reasonable explanation. When no further difficulties with the readings are indicated, the professor asks three different participants questions covering the main aspects of the readings. After each answer, he asks if anyone else in the class has anything to add to the answer given. On two occasions, others in the class comment, mostly in a qualifying way.

Professor Jones then comments briefly on the origin of the case, explaining that a former student happened to sit next to him on an airplane and how they had discussed the course of Professor Jones. Professor Jones had mentioned the difficulties of obtaining new materials on a particular subject and the former student had replied, "That's a coincidence, that is just the problem I'm working on right now. Would you like me to send you information on it?"

Professor Jones then smiles at the class and says, "If there's anything wrong with this case, blame the airline." Then he asks if someone wishes to start the discussion of the first question of the case. The remaining 65 minutes of the class are devoted to the case discussion.

Four people indicate they are ready to start by raising their hands. Professor Jones chooses Frank Carter an infrequent participant in his course so far (and also one of the persons listed on his volunteer preferences list) and Frank starts the class by saying, "... is the key decision that needs to be made. If I were the manager under these circumstances, I would concentrate on this decision because. . ."

Frank then takes about five minutes to explain his reasons and also indicates how he would decide. While he speaks, Professor Jones records key points in summary form on the board. When he finishes, Professor Jones asks him if he has anything more to say. Frank replies, "Oh, yes, there's one point I skipped over." And he recounts it.

Professor Jones turns to the class and already a dozen hands or so are up in the air to indicate they wish to comment. Professor Jones nods to one and that person proceeds to disagree strongly with the key decision identified by Frank. Professor Jones records this counter position on the other side of the board. Before he has a chance to turn away from the board, someone else starts to speak, and the discussion in the class proceeds for about five minutes on the class' own initiative, while Professor Jones continues to record additional points on the board.

It is apparent that a significant segment of the class is in one camp, while the other seems to agree with Frank. Professor Jones then says, "Well, it seems we have reached an impasse, here. If we cannot agree on the issue which needs resolution, there's not much point in going on. Is there any additional information, not yet brought out, which might help in resolving this? I want to hear from someone who has not spoken up so far."

Three persons volunteer and each brings additional information from the case supporting Frank's view. The last person to speak refers to the balance sheet and income statement of the company and Professor Jones uses the projector to show financial statements to allow the participant to comment.

Professor Jones asks if the class agrees on the proper problem definition, and when the class agrees he asks what the basic issues are and the class volunteers about six. He then asks, "Why should we spend class time on these?" and various volunteers explain the relationship of these basic issues to the course and to their future. Next, Professor Jones asks about positioning the main problem in the case on the importance/urgency matrix position and most participants agree the problem is both important and urgent.

Professor Jones next asks the first person on his call list what alternatives can be seriously considered. He offers four alternatives and Professor Jones records these on another board. Discussion then centers on the pros and cons of each and appropriate decision criteria to evaluate these alternatives.

During this period, Professor Jones continues to record new points on the board, asks for clarification, occasionally repeating exactly what someone has said and asks, "Is this what you said?" And, at other times, he paraphrases remarks and asks, "Is this what you intended to say?"

To one student who has already participated four times and appears anxious to break into the discussion, waving his hand energetically and emitting mumbling noises to interrupt others, Professor Jones indicates with a placating hand movement to "cool it." Occasionally, Professor Jones asks someone who does not have a hand up if he or she agrees or disagrees with a particular point but, for the most part, the volunteers have their say. Professor Jones makes sure that people from all parts of the amphitheater classroom have a chance to participate.

Professor Jones moves continually from the board to the center of the room and, occasionally, to one side or another. Once he moves to the very back of the room, asking all to look at the board and to see if they can come up with a conclusion.

About ten minutes are left by the time the four alternatives have been discussed, and Professor Jones asks which one appears more reasonable under the circumstances. With a show of hands from the class it is clear that two of the four choices are "better." Professor Jones asks how to implement each of these. Considerable discussion takes place on the implementation of the first alternative and, with about two minutes to go, Professor Jones says, "Well, I'm sorry, I had hoped we could discuss the implementation of both of these alternatives, because we might see something interesting as a consequence. Unfortunately, we are out of time and we just cannot get into that now. You have covered most of the relevant issues in this case as far as I can see. Congratulations! One thing aside from how to implement the second alternative you may wish to think about: how applicable is this concept to other companies and other industries? I intend to focus more on this implementation stage with you in some of our future classes, because it is an area we need more practice in. Today's topic is one we will not cover specifically in any future classes, but I expect you to be able to use the concept whenever an opportunity presents itself. See you next week."

CHRONOLOGICAL PHASES
IN A CASE DISCUSSION

As can be seen from the description, the reference case class can be divided into certain chronological phases which are directly linked to the Case Teaching Plan (see Exhibit 5-1):

A. In-Class - Pre-Class Set-up
B. Pre-Case Activities
C. Case Discussion
D. Conclusion

A closer look at each of these phases is now in order. It will become quickly evident that what Professor Jones did and what others do may be entirely different. It is useful to recognize the phases and their varied treatments, if for no other reason than identifying the options available to case teachers.

Exhibit 5-1
CHRONOLOGICAL PHASES LINKED TO THE
CASE TEACHING PLAN AGENDA

Chronological Phases	Case Teaching Plan Agenda
A. In-Class / Pre-Class Set-up	
B. Pre-Case Activities	1. Introduction
	2. Next/Other Classes
	3. Comments/Questions
	4. Reading Discussion
	5. Case Introduction
	6. Teaching Aids
C. Case Discussion	7. Assignment Questions
D. Conclusion	8. Conclusion

A. In-Class / Pre-Class Set-up

Professor Jones had a personal habit of arriving a few minutes early in class, just to make sure that he was not late and he did not need to spend class time doing things that could be done before class. Clearing the board, listing the agenda items, re-arranging the furniture, removing debris, working on the notice board, checking the projection equipment, checking the temperature and air quality in the room, and similar tasks are all non-student contact activities which fall into this phase.

He also liked to chat with a few people to catch the "gossip" or class news and to show his interest in what an individual participator or the group was doing and how they fared.

Some instructors like to use this pre-class set-up period to help them in making up their minds whom to call on first. Other instructors have already decided on their call list and volunteer preferences as part of their Case Teaching Plan preparation.

B. Pre-Case Activities

For many case teachers, case discussion does not start immediately as the first item of business on the class agenda. Pre-Case agenda items could include: (1) introduction; (2) next/other classes; (3) comments/ questions; (4) discussion of assigned readings and theoretical concepts; (5) introduction to the case; and (6) teaching aids. All six may not be present in all classes, but each plays a specific role.

1. Introduction. When a professor wishes to start a class, whether a pre-class set-up occurred or not, there is usually considerable noise; people are chatting with one another. A way needs to be found to gain the group's attention and to get down to business. Some professors yell loudly, "Are you ready to go?" Some whistle, some turn on the projection equipment, some just start talking, some use greetings, some just stand and wait. Whatever means are used, it is evident that information from the professor to the class, and vice versa, is not likely to flow without class attention and silence. Professor Jones used a traditional greeting, which the class expected as a signal. He also quickly followed it up with a good news item of interest to the group, the recent soccer victory. He then reviewed the agenda and gave notice of his participation plan.

This practice of announcing at the start of the class which people are on the call list and for what part of the agenda is often called "warm, or soft calling" as opposed to "cold, or hard calling" or "nailing" where no notice is given.

2. Next/Other Classes. The pre-case phase is also a good time to review some points arising out of previous classes, follow-up to previous cases, or theoretical issues; or give notice of special events; or give the assignment for the next or future classes.

Professor Jones used the time right after the introduction to tell the students how some material for future classes could be obtained. He also reminded them of an upcoming field trip. Obviously, his class was already aware of the specific assignments for the next classes because they were part of the course outline and were also accessible from the Internet.

If an assignment for the next class needs to be given, it is usually best to give it near the beginning of the class along with any special instructions since the case discussion may go overtime and the students rush off.

3. *Comments/Questions.* Professor Jones did not have this item on his agenda. The reason for including this section as a possible agenda item is to prevent a major concern of many students from distracting attention to the class. Potential topics could be the rescheduling of the exam period, a visit by a famous person to the school, a governmental change in student financial support, a significant accident or sickness of a classmate or other instructor.

4. *Reading Discussion.* Professor Jones also used the agenda announcement to indicate his intentions for dealing with the readings.

Professor Jones used a significant part of the pre-case activities phase to discuss the readings assigned along with the case. He used two means to check understanding: the opportunity for students to ask questions as well as to ask questions himself. His expectation was that any further deficiencies in theoretical understanding would be caught during the case discussion. Instructors may ask for hand-ins at this point, have a discussion of assigned readings, use a quick quiz, or any other means at their disposal to satisfy themselves that understanding of theory exists.

Unfortunately, the nature of cases often precludes a perfect match between readings and case issues. Thus, it is entirely possible to have a reading assignment pertaining to a previous or future case topic but which is not relevant to the current case.

5. Case Introduction. Professor Jones was able to use a personal anecdote to introduce the case and also draw the participants' attention to his own authorship of the case, implying his own interest and commitment to it. For those who teach their own cases, this introduction is always an available ploy. Since most teachers use cases written by others, they may wish to use other means of reinforcing the necessity for careful attention to the upcoming case discussion. They may wish to review the last few classes to show the sequence leading up to this particular case. They may wish to refer to statements in the media identifying the case problem as an important one for management, or appeal to the group's pride, "Last year's class couldn't make head or tail out of this case, let's see if you can do better."

Along with a planned preview of the case discussion, reinforcement of the importance of the case to the course, the program, management understanding, or society is the second aim of the case introduction. Relevant news items and current events are popular options.

We like the idea of asking during the case introduction which participants in the class have worked in this industry, in this company, or on a similar problem. Then we ask them to describe their experience thereby providing a framework of appreciation for the other participants in the class. Since many cases tend to disclose few data on the industry as a whole, the processes commonly used and the challenges faced by managers, this kind of case introduction not only reinforces the importance of the case and its key issues, but also allows class participants to learn from each other more about the larger context. Participants who tend to be shy about class participation find this a comfortable opportunity to speak in class.

We do not like, however, the idea of having a student start by summarizing the key facts of the case. For us, this kind of start is the "kiss of death" and signals another boring session. Participants are expected to come to class fully prepared to address the issues and challenges in the case.

6. Teaching Aids. Professor Jones used no teaching aids, although as case author it should have been relatively easy for him to request an annual report, a video, a product or service brochure, some samples or some other teaching aid to reinforce the reality of the case and increase student interest.

C. The Case Discussion

7. The Assignment Questions. Professor Jones started the Case Discussion phase by using the assignment questions. He asked for volunteers for his first question and he had a call list for his second one. Both questions were decision-based and students were expected to use the standard process outlined in the Case Preparation Chart.

A "normal" case discussion is supposed to follow more or less the typical decision making model discussed in Chapter 3 of *Learning with Cases.* This model includes:

a. defining the issue;
b. analyzing the case data with focus on causes and effects as well as constraints and opportunities;
c. generating alternatives;
d. selecting decision criteria;
e. analyzing and evaluating alternatives;
f. selecting the preferred alternative; and
g. developing an action and implementation plan.

Many students like to announce their decision at the start, therefore, the class discussion does not always proceed as the decision making model would. (Fully prepared, the students should have covered all phases of the model prior to class. Therefore, the class is not intended to be a sample of the decision making model). Also, since ease of implementation should be a consideration in the attractiveness of various alternatives, (difficulty to implement cuts down on practicability), implementation considerations need to be discussed before a final decision on the better alternatives is taken. Nevertheless, in many case classes, implementation discussion is left to the end of class, on the assumption that action/implementation planning will not be so difficult as to make the preferred alternative(s) impractical.

Since the central thrust in most case discussions is a resolution of the specific decision or problem in the organization, four distinct segments in a case discussion are:

1. start
2. issues and analysis
3. alternatives, decision criteria and decision and
4. action/implementation plan.

1. Start. Starting the case discussion implies the professor will ask someone to reply to an assigned question and will allocate a certain amount of time to that individual. Professor Jones asked for a volunteer for his first question, and was prepared to let the participant continue until the participant felt he had no more to say.

There are two major types of questions with which to start a class. The extremes are directive and non-directive. A directive question could be, "How much profit do you think this company will make next year?" A non-directive question, particularly appropriate if no case assignment questions were provided could be, "What would you like to talk about?"

We feel strongly that if the students have been given specific questions as part of the case assignment, those questions need to be discussed in class. Thus, suppose the first assignment question is, "If you were in the position of Angela Martins, what would be your analysis of the sales shortfall in the eastern part of the country?" Then it is perfectly reasonable and desirable to make that the opening question for class discussion. Instructors who do not believe the case assignment questions need to be discussed in class had better communicate this to the class to avoid frustration and confusion.

Of course there is a general understanding that it is possible for participants and the instructor to raise points outside of the questions assigned. There is a difference whether these extra points and insights are in addition to the assignment questions or a substitute for them.

2. Issues and Analysis At some stage of the class discussion, normally, but not always, in the early stages, considerable discussion takes place to identify the exact nature of the immediate issue, problem or decision in the case. Discussion of alternatives and implementation is rather meaningless without common agreement in the class that the right issue is being addressed. For this reason, Professor Jones in our reference class forced the class to resolve its differences before allowing further discussion. In some cases, the task of identifying the prime decision or problem is trivial and need not consume much time. In others, the central educational issue may well be the proper identification of the correct problem. How much time to allot to this phase will, therefore, depend on the objectives the instructor has for the class and the nature of the case.

It is also useful to have the class determine what the basic issues are to remind them of the relevance of the case to the course and their potential future career. Similarly, the positioning of the issues in this case on the importance/urgency matrix assists in establishing priorities, alternatives, decision criteria, and developing an action/implementation plan. It was obvious from Professor Jones' class that his questions about the basic issues and importance/urgency matrix were expected by his class and were quickly dealt with.

Case analysis can start after the development of the issue and its importance and urgency. Understanding why the issue arose and why it is relevant to the course provides both motivation and insight essential to effective quantitative and qualitative analyses in the course. The analytical framework and theoretical concepts of the specific course are expected to tie into the analysis of the case.

It is important to reinforce that in this text and in *Learning with Cases* the only framework provided is the decision making/problem solving model. Every instructor needs to add for his or her own course those analytical tools and theoretical concepts which pertain to the specific field of study. Every case class affords an opportunity to combine the general problem solving model with the course specific analytical tools to address the real life issues presented in the case. Whereas the reading discussion part of the class may focus on a specific theory or concept, the analytical part of the case discussion permits testing of a much broader band of theoretical perspectives both in understanding and application.

"Time-outs" to depart from the case and go back to earlier classes and concepts are usual. If the case is of the type where something did not work out as planned, the fishbone or cause and effect diagram can provide a suitable framework for establishing potential root causes. The prime purpose of the case analysis section in the class discussion is to ensure that any alternatives which are subsequently generated are appropriate for the decision or issue under consideration. The medical analysis equivalent is proper diagnosis before prescription.

3. Alternatives, Decision Criteria and Decision. A significant part of any case class deals with the discussion of alternatives. Sometimes, even before the decision or problem is clearly identified, alternatives or solutions are already proposed by the class members. Normally, at least two, and sometimes up to a dozen alternatives are advanced by participants. The larger the number of alternatives, the greater the need is for narrowing or shortening this list before serious discussion of the merits of the most important ones can take place.

Any time a list needs to be made in class, such as for alternatives, or decision criteria, it is useful to ensure that all potential possibilities are listed before discussion of appropriateness or advantages/disadvantages can begin. Thus, the instructor can say, "Let me get the full set of options down first, before we start discussing them." Otherwise, someone will present an alternative with or without a lot of supporting arguments, and then someone else will start to argue with the pros and cons. Under this scenario it is quite possible that a much better alternative not yet identified gets a short or no discussion while some less worthy options take up valuable class time.

The list of alternatives can be reduced in a variety of ways. One option is to ask for a class vote on each alternative and discuss only the more popular ones. The instructor may also ask the class to distinguish between the alternatives. That is, ask which apply specifically to the situation versus good ideas which should be carried out regardless of the particular situation at hand. For example, in one case where a significant rise in raw material prices is forecast, students typically suggest changing package size. In this particular case, this suggestion in itself may be a reasonable auxiliary action, but it will not solve the raw material price increase.

Also, to narrow the number of alternatives, an instructor can ask which alternatives are based on an assumption which has a low probability of success. In the price situation above, finding a substitute material is frequently another alternative proposed. The relevant question that needs to be asked is, "What is the probability that a substitute exists and that it is available at a lower cost than the increased price of the raw material?"

Further, which alternatives can be eliminated because there are others already identified which appear to have superior pay-off?

For the same example discussed above, the raw material is currently purchased from the parent company in England at an advantageous price. The alternative of purchasing it elsewhere in Great Britain and obtaining a better price is not very realistic, given the specific circumstances.

It is also possible to discuss one attractive alternative in some depth and thus establish a "reference base" alternative, against which others can be compared.

For example, in the above case, continuing to buy from the parent company will cost the subsidiary about $4,000,000 per year more. Therefore, any other alternative, to be attractive, will have to cost less, and the size of the problem is clearly identified. It is a $4,000,000 problem, not a $400,000 one, or a $40,000 one. Therefore, the solutions have to fit that problem.

After the narrowing down of alternatives, the serious examination of the two or three most attractive ones can begin.

Some instructors prefer to have board space reserved for alternatives; others do not. It is useful to record the key alternatives and their pros and cons on the board, or overhead projector or flip chart, for the group to see, so that discussion can be more reasonably managed.

Decision Criteria. A listing of decision criteria usually follows on the heels of an alternative listing or may precede it. Criteria subsequently need to be separated into quantitative and qualitative categories. *Learning with Cases* gives a list of common decision criteria in Chapter 3. Next, both the quantitative and qualitative criteria need to be prioritized. It is most unusual for everyone in class to be in full agreement with such rankings. Therefore, it is better to ask one participant to provide a ranking and then to ask, "How many agree with this ranking?" and "How many disagree?" Then ask one of those who disagree to provide his or her own ranking. It is also useful to ask if the quantitative criteria should outweigh the qualitative ones or vice versa. If this is done well, it can then form the basis for alternative evaluation.

Alternative Evaluation. Discussion of the alternatives should normally focus on one alternative at a time. The instructor records the pros and cons against the established criteria so that subsequent class comparison between alternatives is possible.

It may well be that in any case more than one alternative is fully reasonable, even after careful examination. Such was the situation in the class of Professor Jones. It is usually wise to ask participants to state their reasons for their choice, so that their line of logic is clear and reasonable. The argument of, "The key objective is to lower cost, and alternative 'B' appears to have the best chance of achieving a significantly lower cost," is logical. However, "Alternative 'B' is better because delivery is faster," is not reasonable under these circumstances.

It is during the alternatives discussion stage that relevant data from the case normally need to be brought in to bolster the pros and cons of each alternative as well as the key decision criteria. The instructor may well ask the class to check back to specific pages in the case and may have diagrams, charts, statements, or calculations available which can be projected on the screen.

Toward the end of the case discussion phase, it is usually necessary to reach a conclusion as to the "best alternative(s)." Class consensus may be obvious, or may be solicited by a question, "How many believe this to be the best alternative?" or an individual may be asked to make a choice and others to agree or disagree.

If part of the objective of this class is to discuss an action/implementation plan, sufficient time should be left, a problem Professor Jones could not quite resolve.

4. Action/Implementation Plan. Discussion of an action/implementation plan often receives scant attention in case classes, because many instructors believe proper identification and analysis of the problem and discussion of theory are more important. Also, since implementation is logically a discussion area restricted to the end of the class, a race with the clock is frequently lost. Such was the case with Professor Jones who admitted to the class his own inability to manage time better.

Since an action/implementation plan, including deadlines, is better viewed as an integral whole, it is usually preferable to have a person who agrees with the preferred alternative provide a whole action/implementation plan rather than just one or two steps. Then, others may advance an alternative action/implementation plan, or suggest additional or different steps and deadlines. Since ease, cost and time of implementation are obvious decision criteria for any alternative, the opportunity to revisit the list of alternatives once an action/implementation plan runs into trouble needs to be foreseen.

Instructors who believe that the ability to prepare a decent action/implementation plan is a valuable skill to be learned by their course participants had better be prepared to set a significant amount of class time aside for discussion of this phase. They would do well to emphasize to participants in their case assignment that they expect to discuss a serious action/implementation plan, so that participants can prepare properly. A hastily conceived action/implementation plan in class cobbled together from about a dozen contributors is likely to fall significantly short of its quality goal. What is worse, is that a half-baked plan may give the participants the idea that this is a decent effort and set an undesirable standard of expectations.

D. Conclusion

"Oh, I see my time's up. I look forward to our next class," is probably the shortest but not the least likely conclusion an instructor can give to the end of a case class. Like the class start, it is a transition phase, which can be used to conclude the case and provide a transition to subsequent classes as well as a continuation in the sequence so far completed.

Some instructors prefer that students summarize the case. Most feel that asking a student to conclude is a difficult role to perform. Some instructors like to wrap-up the case and its key points themselves, perhaps commenting also on strengths and weaknesses in the class discussion of the case. Those who strongly believe in non-directive behavior prefer to leave the responsibility for evaluation of what happened in class and why on the shoulders of the participants and do not summarize or comment. Professor Jones was rather noncommittal and passed very quickly from the case, just warning that the topic would not be repeated.

It is also possible in these final moments to cover theory, reinforce earlier classes, preview subsequent ones, and to give the participants a lift at the end of the class. Often, relatively strong feelings may have emerged and some humorous remarks or quiet discussion can provide a calming influence before the session ends.

Most instructors feel the need for some type of closure at the end of a class. It is difficult, in their opinion, to walk away leaving the discussion completely in the open. The answers to the question, "How do you end a class?" show there are many useful things that instructors can do to help students develop a broader understanding from specific case situations and to enrich their learning experience. For example, instructors may wish to provide some conceptual input in the form of a lecture to review some important points raised in the discussion; highlight certain aspects of the case; raise questions regarding some points missed; or indicate some pitfalls with each of the alternatives identified.

Congratulating the class on a job well done should only be considered for those occasions where the instructor honestly feels this to be true. A phony compliment will lower the esteem the class may hold for the instructor and lower future quality expectations.

Disagreement exists as to whether instructors should summarize at the end of the class or not. Personal teaching style and philosophy as well as the type of course and nature of participants are all factors which influence conclusion preferences.

There are two further ways of ending class which, although often relished by students, should be handled with care. One is for the instructor to provide his or her own solution to the case and the other is to tell the class what the company actually did.

The first approach may be risky in several ways. A few students may reject or challenge the instructor's solution in an unproductive fashion while a large number may accept it as the "correct" one. Also, if students expect the instructor to provide "the answer" at the end of the class, it may well demotivate them to search extensively for their own alternatives and turn them towards trying to predict which alternative the instructor will favor. That is not the purpose of the case method. It would be wise for the instructor, when offering an opinion about a case, to caution students that it is an opinion and not the answer. Some instructors prefer to state such opinions informally after class is over.

Sometimes, especially when an instructor has written the case, there may be great temptation to reveal what the company actually did. Of course, confidences and disguises should never be violated and students should understand that the company's decision was not necessarily the best solution. Also, news of this sort tends to provide closure to the case. Some case instructors insist that the mind keeps working away on unresolved problems much longer than on situations where the instructor has told students what actually happened in the company. Finally, it implies that the instructor is privy to additional information the student does not have about the situation. The idea that "all of us enter the situation with equal information, let us explore it together" does not really hold.

We believe it is useful to remind students to take no more than five minutes immediately after class to record and summarize their own key observations, insights or generalizations on their Case Preparation Chart (see *Learning with Cases*, Chapter 5).

THE PARTICIPATIVE PROCESS

Throughout the case discussion the instructor faces a variety of issues not necessarily related to the specific case, but concerned with managing the participative process according to the Class Teaching Plan. These issues will be discussed next. All of them focus on what the instructor can do in the classroom. They deal with topics such as questioning and responding, recording contributions, instructor movement and voice control, managing participation, dealing with participation problems, dealing with material problems, pushing for decision and implementation, managing time and sequence, maintaining order, dealing with trade-offs and using humor in case discussions.

The art of leading a case discussion involves questioning, listening and responding. Questioning means asking the right question at the right time. Questioning includes the type and number of questions the instructor asks to elicit appropriate class coverage of the case as well as the timing of these questions. Listening is the bridge between questioning and responding. Responding refers to the instructor's actions after participant comments.

Questioning

The ideal model of the instructor as a skillful questioner would have the instructor question so naturally that the participants would hardly be aware of it. That would be quite a contrast to the instructor looking helplessly at the class and saying, "I don't know where we go from here, can anybody help us out?" Even though in the case method this question could be appropriate, it is one that should probably be used sparingly.

The use of the appropriate question at the right time to keep the case discussion moving properly is a valuable skill every instructor must acquire. Questions can be divided into two main categories: generic and case specific.

Generic Questions. Generic questions could theoretically be used by an instructor who has not even read the case. Every once in a while we have heard of an instructor who has tried conducting a class without any knowledge of the case itself.

Clearly, this is not a recommended practice. However, it would be one way of sharpening one's generic questioning skills. Generic questions include a number of discussion process questions focusing on clarification, length of contribution, who speaks and timing. Good case teachers use almost instinctively process questions like: "Why?", "Is this what you said?", "Who would like to speak next?", and "Are there any further points anyone wishes to make?"

Other generic questions can be linked to the analytical, conceptual and presentation dimensions of the Case Difficulty Cube. Analytical questions cover the full spectrum of the Case Preparation Chart. For example, a simple generic analytical question is: "What is the problem decision, issue or challenge?" Conceptual questions relate to the specific theoretical content of the course. A generic conceptual question is: "What theory applies to this situation?" Presentation questions are concerned with what information is available and where. A generic presentation question is: "Where in the case is there support for your statement?"

The question list shown in Exhibit 5-2 classifies generic questions into four categories. The first category includes the generic discussion process questions that every case teacher brings to every class and is ready to use as the occasion requires.

The remaining three categories cover the analytical, conceptual and presentation dimensions of the Case Difficulty Cube.

Case Specific Questions. Case specific questions have already been discussed as part of the teaching note under the heading: Potential Discussion Questions for Use in Class. They are meant to be particularly useful questions to raise in class, should students not have addressed these topics as part of the normal class discussion.

Many case specific questions can be directly extended from the generic analytical, conceptual and presentation questions listed in Exhibit 5-2. For example: "What in your analysis?" could change to "What do the financial

Exhibit 5-2
GENERIC QUESTIONS DURING CASE DISCUSSION

Generic Process Questions

- Why? Can you explain it differently?
- Would you mind repeating what you just said?
- Would you like to add anything to what you have said?
- Is this what you meant to say?
- Do you agree/disagree with what X said?
- Who would like to speak next?
- Who has something different/new to add to what has already been said?
- Who would like to summarize?/conclude?
- Is it time to move on?
- How much time do we have left?
- Do we have enough time to ….?

Generic Analytical Questions

- What is the issue?
- What position are we supposed to hold?
- Why did this issue arise?
- By when does it have to be resolved?
- What is (are) the immediate issue(s)?
- What is (are) the basic issue(s)?
- How important is this issue?
- How urgent is this issue?
- What is your analysis?
- What alternatives do you suggest?
- What are your decision criteria?
- What is the best alternative?
- What outcome do you predict?
- What is your action/implementation plan?

Generic Conceptual Questions

- Which theory(ies) concept(s), tool(s) or technique(s) is (are) applicable, useful?
- Which theory(ies) might be relevant?
- Who can explain what the relevant theory(ies), concept(s), technique(s) is (are)?
- What have you learned in this course (other courses) this year (in previous years) that might be applicable?
- What does the textbook (article, reading) say?

Generic Presentation Questions

- What information is there in the case to support this?
- Where in the case is there information regarding this?
- What information in the case is relevant to this issue? Not relevant?
- What information is missing?
- What assumptions have you made?

statements in Exhibit 2 reveal?" And, "What theories or concepts might be useful?" could change to "What do you think the break-even point would be if this product were priced at $7.50?" And, "What information is missing?" could change to "How would you find out at what price the current owner might be willing to sell the business?"

While case specific questions will always require teacher review, even when an instructor teaches the same case repeatedly, generic questions become a part of the teacher's subconscious skill set, used when and as required.

Listening

Listening means much more than just hearing the words. It also means evaluating the speaker's understanding and use of case information as well as the speaker's contribution to the discussion process. We tell students that the secret to effective participation in a case discussion is to listen and think at the same time. The same can be said for leading an effective discussion. While the student makes a contribution, the instructor must listen, understand, reflect and decide how to respond.

Silence also plays a role. After a participant has spoken or the instructor has asked a question, it may be appropriate to let silence reign. Even half a minute may seem like an eternity, but not every second of every class needs to be filled by the spoken word. Students and instructors alike may need some time for reflection. Knowing when to speak and when to keep silent, and for how long, is part of the wisdom of participative teaching.

A student may talk for 4-5 minutes and there may be a dozen points the instructor can respond to. Picking the right one, so that the instructor can move the discussion in the way he or she wants and also in a way that indicates the student has made a point worth expanding on, is not easy. Moreover, the teacher has to learn to listen selectively so that he or she can be thinking. Where do I want to go next with the discussion while this speaker is holding forth?

Responding

A skill parallel to questioning in managing the participative process is to be able to respond to what students say.

Responding means for the instructor to choose between multiple alternatives: (1) repeating and clarifying what the current speaker has just contributed; (2) probing or elaborating for further commentary; (3) paraphrasing; (4) summarizing to close some issue before moving on; (5) transitioning to shift the discussion or linking to build the discussion; (6) challenging the speaker to see the other side of the argument; (7) thanking and acknowledging the speaker; (8) evaluating; (9) informing or commenting to interpret some facts or emphasize some point; (10) interrupting; (11) non-verbal responses; and (12) recording to validate the contribution and retain the idea for future reference or analysis.

1. Repeating and Clarifying. One of the simplest responses a case instructor may give is, "Would you please repeat what you have just said?" The class may be noisy and/or the participant may speak in such a low voice that he or she is barely audible. Thus, "Would you please repeat and a bit louder?" is also a frequent response. Occasionally, the repeat response may be used to emphasize a particularly important point or insight that deserves reinforcement.

Clarification falls between paraphrasing and repeating. "Is this what you said?" represents an attempt by the instructor to repeat exactly what the participant said in his or her own words. If the instructor uses different words from those of the participant, clarification becomes paraphrasing.

2. Probing or Elaborating Responses. A common challenge for instructors is to deal with participants who are too succinct in their comments. "I think the first alternative is the best." Now the task of extracting the reasoning process begins for the instructor: "Why?" or "Can you give me the reasons why you think the first alternative is the best?" Are your reasons quantitative or qualitative?" or "What are the key advantages of the first alternative?"

The instructor engages in a series of questions of the "tell me more" variety to ensure that the participant's reasoning is understood by all.

Even for participants who are more capable of contributing in multiple sentences, the elaborative responses from the instructor and occasionally from fellow students are useful to ensure common understanding. "Why?" and "Please explain further." and "Is there anything else you wish to add?" are three of the most common and useful types.

3. Paraphrasing Responses. Paraphrasing responses from instructors are semi-evaluative in the sense that the instructor believes the point(s) made by a participant would be better understood if expressed in different words. For example, "In other words, are you saying that pricing this product at this low price would mean this product would have to achieve 40 percent market share to break-even?"

4. Summarizing Responses. A summarizing response by an instructor can be used at various stages of the class discussion, including the conclusion. In the simplest sense summarizing is almost always used during the recording of a contribution, "Can I summarize your views by saying this option (or alternative) is too expensive?" "Therefore, are you for or against this option?" is a way to cut short a verbose participant.

At the end of the discussion of an assignment question or a key aspect of the case, the instructor may ask a participant to summarize the previous discussion, "Who can summarize what has been said so far about this alternative, analysis, situation …?", or the instructor may wish to summarize, "Now that we have had a chance to think about and discuss this question, it seems we are in reasonable agreement that we cannot let the current situation go on much longer and that we have to find a solution to this problem."

Summarizing at the end of the class, if done by the instructor, may review the major contributions made, "You may wish to reflect on what Mary, Peter and Pearl had to say about this case, because …"

Quite differently, the instructor may choose to reinforce major learning points, "Notice, a pricing decision cannot be made in a vacuum. Key other considerations are: …"

5. *Transitioning and Linking Responses.* Transitioning responses are attempts to move the discussion to another speaker or to another topic. "Let us see what Mary has to say about this", or "Who would like to add something to this specific issue?", and "I think we have spent enough time on this point, let's move to another."

In classes with many participants eager to participate, the instructor may wish to establish a sequence: "Ethel first, then John and then Lee." Given that a good case class is built on a large variety of contributions from different individuals, part of the instructor's contribution is the assurance of a sequential logic as well as a reinforcement of the whole. The class is collectively contributing to a construction project.

Linking responses by the instructor assure that there will be cement and glue and other fasteners to assure the structure will not fall apart. A typical response of this type would be, "How does what you are saying relate to what the previous speakers have said?" The instructor may be involved in linking not only one point of the discussion to another point, but one class to another class, one course section to another section, one course to other courses, and even one course to a total program. In doing so, the professor supplies the glue that makes the whole thing stick together.

It is critical for students to have it clear in their mind every day where they are on this intellectual journey they are taking. Besides outlines and notes on the course, an instructor should spend time periodically to state, "Here's where we've been, here's where we are and here's where we're going."

It is useful also to keep raising old cases. Some instructors try to remember who took what position in certain cases. It really impresses students to say, "Tina took this position in last week's case, now relate it to this situation." The instructor can encourage more learning because suddenly students begin to think, "There's something important going on; somebody's listening to what I'm saying."

6. *Challenging Responses.* A challenging response encourages a participant to elucidate on the opposite side of his or her arguments. "Now argue the other side. What are the negative factors?" This response is often used with

an assumption: "Suppose your assumption does not hold and there is not a lot of money available, then how would that affect your comments, conclusion, recommendation?"

7. *Acknowledging Responses.* A common and courteous instructor acknowledging response to a participant's class contribution in addition to a single head nod is a simple "Thank you" or "Thank you for your contribution."

8. *Evaluative Responses.* It is possible for an instructor to act as evaluator of the comments made by the participant. On the negative side, "I don't think you have the facts straight" or "Do you really mean what you are saying?" (where the tone is one of incredulity.)

On the positive side the instructor can say: "This is a very good comment" or "What a good start" or "Congratulations, this is the best analysis I have ever seen."

Another way of evaluating is for the instructor to refuse to record the contribution or at least hesitate to do so. A different evaluative response is to switch quickly to another participant without inviting the speaker to elaborate or expand on his or her views.

Many instructors believe that making evaluative responses in class turns the participative process into a one-on-one exchange with the instructor and the participant in which the goal of the participant is to obtain the instructor's approval. Therefore, instructors will try to avoid arguing the merits of specific contributions with only an exceptional positive or negative response. Thus, the instructor records all comments, good or bad, and explains at the beginning of the course that he or she expects participants themselves to agree or disagree with specific points spoken or recorded.

Similarly, in class discussion the instructor will appear equally solicitous and supportive of the participant who argues a highly doubtful position as the one who appears to be right on track.

9. Informing Responses. The case instructor always has the option of responding in an informative sense on the case itself or the basic issue or theoretical perspective: "Well, when I visited this company (or a similar company or when I read the article or looked at the website), I found out that the ratio of office to plant workers was about 1 to 15."

The instructor may wish to launch into a mini-lecture or review the readings or other theoretical or conceptual material, "Let us just step out of the case for a few minutes. What did the readings suggest as a way to analyze this issue?" or "Can anyone explain what X (the current guru on the subject) has to contribute to this issue?" or "Let me try to explain what this theory really tries to do" or "What did we learn three classes ago about the proper application of this technique?"

A common way to reinforce case or issue relevance is to quote current news items from the various media: "This issue of executive compensation was highlighted in ..."

10. Interrupting Responses. If a participant is taking a long time to explain a simple point or is far from clear in his or her language, the instructor may wish to interrupt and offer a summarizing, paraphrasing or clarifying response: "Please let me stop you right there, is this what you are trying to say?"

11. Non-Verbal Responses. Non-verbal responses are constantly used by instructors in addition to or as substitutes for verbal responses. Smiling is a friendly response, frowning is not. Nodding the head in encouragement and hand movements to quieten the class or elicit elaboration or point to the next speaker serve as quick indicators as to what should happen next. All responses, verbal and non-verbal, have both a cultural context as well as evidence of the personal style of the instructor. Thus, other relevant references in this chapter include the sections on instructor movement, the use of humor and teaching style.

12. Recording Responses. By recording the contribution of a participant the instructor is normally reinforcing the worth of the contribution. The greater the amount of board space or the longer the record, the better the contribution must be. Thus, recording contribution serves as a reward for the participant. In classrooms with limited board space it may not be possible to retain all contributions on the board and the nasty question arises as to whose contributions will be erased. The instructor may wish to say, "Please don't feel offended if I erase your comments", as he or she vigorously wipes the board clean of valuable contributions.

Since recording also requires summarizing and paraphrasing, some responses such as, "Is it okay to write (summarize) it this way?" or "Have I recorded your comment(s) correctly?" serve as a feedback loop.

Questioning and Responding Combinations

Certain questions and responses tend to occur frequently in combinations. For example when an instructor asks a student to volunteer, the following combination of initial question and follow on responses is typical:

1. Who would like to start the class?
2. What do you wish to talk about?
3. What do you mean by that?

4. Is there anything else you would like to say? (Before I turn to someone else.)

5. Who would like to take it from here? or, Who agrees with what has been said? or, Who disagrees with what has been said? or, Who would like to add something to what has just been said?

This combination is often used in a non-directive style start. (For a discussion of teaching style, please refer to this topic at the end of this chapter.)

If a specific student is asked to answer an assignment question the combination could be:

1. Chris, will you please answer the next question?

2. Did you do any calculations?

3. What do your figures show?

4. Is it possible you might interpret this data differently?

5. Why do you believe that this is a viable alternative?

6. What are your decision criteria?

7. What is your qualitative analysis?

8. How would you implement what you are recommending?

This example would show a more directive style in a situation where the same student is expected to connect, analysis, decision and implementation.

Recording Contributions

Every instructor needs to come to terms with his or her recording role in class, "Do I include in my role the job of 'class discussion secretary'?" If the answer is no, then it is safe to assume that no record of class comments will be made. We have encountered attempts by instructors to have a scribe record on the board the comments of various class members. Invariably, the scribe falls behind or fails to record what the instructor would like to see on the board and the instructor may find it difficult to refer to previous points. If the scribe is another faculty member or an assistant, resource costs increase significantly. If the scribe is a student volunteer or conscript, that individual loses the opportunity to participate in the class discussion. For these reasons instructors normally include the recording task within their teaching role.

Most instructors believe it is helpful, at least for themselves, and normally as well for their participants, to maintain a visual record of key points made during the class. There are some cases, particularly in the organizational behavior area, where few points need to be visually recorded. However, recording slows down the discussion and it is not possible to record everything. Therefore, the instructor has to be selective and "reward" some students by recognizing their contribution while ignoring others. The positive aspect of recording contributions is that a combination of audio and visual reinforcement provides a common reference and easier recall throughout the discussion.

Various devices such as black or white or electronic boards, flip charts, overhead projectors and screens may be used during this process. How well the instructor records affects the quality of class discussion.

Boards. Boards are probably the most common recording means available for case discussion and serve a number of functions. The most important are: a focal point where class comments are recorded; a tool to structure the discussion; a reinforcer; and a way of clarifying points, calculations or explanations.

As part of the recording function, one question is whether the instructor should put on the board the student's own words or summarize and interpret these words. Once again, it depends on what the instructor is trying to achieve. Many instructors like to be exact in their reporting for fear of biases or too much interference. For these people, recording is merely a means for keeping the key elements of the discussion before the class. Nonetheless, it should be recognized that by recording something that has been said, implicit reinforcement takes place.

It is always necessary to use some form of shorthand because there is never enough time and space to record comments verbatim. Even with shorthand, very few boards are large enough to be able to handle an entire class discussion. For this reason, it will be necessary to erase some ideas, or hide them behind if sliding boards are available. Knowing this, the instructor may be subconsciously trying to economize on board space. This may well mean that refusing to record a weak contribution becomes tempting. Even a momentary hesitation will signal to the class that here is something the instructor may not be too keen on recording. If the instructor wishes to encourage the class to take issue with the point raised, the class had better be aware of this desire. A comment like, "All I will do is record ideas on the board, you are responsible for evaluating them," is useful under these circumstances.

As suggested in the Case Teaching Plan it is useful to plan and work out ahead of time any charts, diagrams or calculations required on the board to avoid embarrassing situations Colors can be used to highlight and relate important points by underlining and circling them in the same color.

Legibility of the comments on the board and an understanding of the shorthand used by the instructor are important. It is a good idea for the instructors to walk occasionally to the back of the class and look at the board to see if it is possible to read what has been recorded.

Instructors do not always realize how much time is required for the students to take proper notes. By writing the major points on the board, it enables the teacher to hold down his or her own speed to the rest of the class.

A major disadvantage of the board is that the instructor needs to turn his or her back to the class. The overhead projector solves part of this problem.

Overhead Projection. Many of the comments which apply to the board use also apply to the overhead projector. In addition to enabling the instructor to face the class continually, the overhead projector has other distinctive attributes over the board.

The instructor is able to use materials prepared ahead of time, which is a great advantage, especially for people with bad handwriting, and therefore, speed up the process. It is not necessary to erase comments already made. It is possible to go back and review all of the recordings for a total class and even to distribute them to the students, allowing them to concentrate in class on the discussion, instead of on taking notes. In hotels, or other such locations where it is practically impossible to get a decent board, it may well be the only reasonable alternative, provided a large enough screen is available. There are no limits as to how sophisticated one can be in his or her use of charts and slides.

There is a danger, however, in using too many prepared overhead transparencies or Power Point slides. The students may feel the instructor wants to lecture and cut down on their class participation.

Moreover, the overhead projector is not a panacea. It is difficult for the instructor to stare at the light and the class at the same time; and it draws the attention of the students somewhat excessively to the front of the class when they should be focussing on each other. It works better at focussing on specific points than at providing a global picture for a discussion.

Electronic Projection. Electronic projection offers on-line in class use of the computer to bring in Internet provided information, instant calculations based on different "what if" scenarios, in addition to prepared presentations.

One disadvantage of electronic projection is the recording task is not as easily handled as with boards or overhead projection. Therefore, most case instructors tend to use a combination of projection means and boards depending on options available in a particular classroom.

Instructor Movement and Voice Control

The role of the instructor in the case class is not at all limited to questions and responses and recording as discussed so far. The way the questions and responses are made and the accompanying body language of the instructor speak volumes about the instructor's enthusiasm, interest and support.

In the reference class discussion, Professor Jones moved throughout the classroom, although he spent most of his time at the board or near the center of the room. Effective body movement can assist the instructor in performing almost all of the various tasks identified in managing the case discussion.

Furthermore, effective use of voice level and speed of speaking can reinforce the educational message the instructor is trying to convey. The way questions are asked will also send a message. A firm tone and aggressive body stance convey quite a different message from a gentle tone and a relaxed body language.

By moving toward a student, the instructor is likely to have the student conclude his or her contribution faster, while moving slowly away is likely to have the opposite effect. By turning his or her back to a section of the class the instructor sends a message, "I don't wish to hear from you now." The speed of movement and speech of the instructor will also affect the tempo of the class. Hand signals and a nod of the head may encourage or discourage participation and transition of the discussion from one person to another.

The instructor not only sends non-verbal signals, but also receives them. By paying attention to eye contact, noise level, body positions or side remarks, the instructor may realize it is time to re-orient the discussion, to change the pace or to conclude.

Some instructors have found it useful to take acting lessons to reinforce effective body and voice use. An instructor should not try to make a major point while moving rapidly. Stand still instead and speak slowly and loudly. The dramatic use of voice and movement can change an ordinary class into an exceptional one.

Managing Participation

There are many ways an instructor can deal with the management of participation in the classroom. The choice of whom to call on first and what to pose as the starting question have been discussed previously.

The decision on whom to call on and whom to give preference to during the remainder of the discussion phases needs further coverage.

When there is more than one hand up in class and none of the potential contributors are among the instructor's volunteer preferences, whom should the instructor call on? The one having it up the longest? The one waving frantically? The person who has not recently spoken? The person who said the previous evening, "I'm going to really be ready tomorrow?"

There is still the question regarding contribution norms. Will participants signal by putting up their hand? Will they keep it up while someone is talking? Will waving help? Should the instructor indicate: "Sally is next, followed by Karl and Tom Lee?" Can anyone interrupt the discussion or should everything flow through the instructor? It is often a sign of a good class discussion that the class itself will carry on the discussion without instructor direction. This happened in Professor Jones' class and he quietly recorded points without inserting himself into the discussion. By walking to the back of the class the instructor sends a message, "You are on your own. Carry on." Every case instructor needs to develop a set of norms for classroom participation acceptable to him or herself as well as the class.

Dealing with Participation Problems

Part of the instructor's task in managing participation is to deal with four types of problems: low, poor, overactive and dysfunctional participation.

In this chapter, the focus will lie with what the instructor might do in the classroom about these problems. Further follow-up on an individual or small group basis in the office may be required and will be discussed in Chapter 7. Low participation, in particular, is unlikely to be resolved adequately by classroom measures alone.

Low Participation. In any class, there will always be some people who participate little or not at all. In an 80-minute class, it is difficult to have more than 30 people participate in the discussion in a meaningful way. Therefore, if the class size is larger than this or the time available is less, a number of people can obviously not participate. The problem is to prevent the same people from not participating in every class. Part of the difficulty is that with a participative method like the case method, any repetitive non-participant can become isolated from the group and feelings of non-involvement and frustration begin. Some may try to "psych themselves up" to participate in a class. If they succeed, they will probably feel better. If they do not, they will feel even worse. In the latter case, a spiral may start to the point that individuals may find it becomes impossible to work; every class becomes a mountain of trouble and real feelings of depression occur.

The correlation between ability and willingness to participate is not always obvious. Many poor students volunteer frequently, while the good ones sit silently. There are a number of actions instructors can take in class to help low or non-participators.

Calling on a low participator with or without prior notice is the most common option used by instructors to ensure participation. Prior notice "softens" the impact and asking a question which should be easy for the particular student is also a gentle initiation.

Some instructors after two or three classes in the course ask that only those who have not yet had a chance to speak up in class carry the discussion. This can probably only be done relatively early into a course, and it certainly pinpoints the individuals involved, which may well carry some heavy penalties.

Another option is to put all of the names of people in the class in a small hat, basket or large cup and have someone draw names to establish the order of participation. It tends to create a bit of a strained discussion, because it lacks the spontaneity and natural flow of a more volunteer-based discussion.

Another choice is to say, "Everyone is going to make at least one statement about this case, and it may not be a repetition of what anyone else has said, nor repetition of a case fact without an evaluation or implication attached." Then, asking every second or third person in a row to talk moves the discussion quickly over the whole class. This works reasonably well, except the instructor tends to run out of board space and comments run the full gamut from problem definition through analysis, alternatives, etc. to implementation. Sequence will be non-existent. The net result, generally, is a reasonable assessment of almost everything in the case, but disorganized and the instructor may have to provide broad concluding remarks.

It is also possible to ask students themselves to choose their own successor after their own participation.

On reflection, it may well be that the real benefit of these kinds of efforts lies more with the reinforcement that participation is important, than with the technique itself.

Poor Participation. It is possible for students to participate, but not in the desired spirit and quality. They may not have prepared properly and remarks may be shallow or off the mark. As discussed in Chapter 4, the instructor must indicate the quality of work expected and insist that the class live up to these norms.

Regular acceptance of poor quality participation will bring the whole class down to a mediocre level. At times, it may be necessary to resort to other means. For example, it is possible to ask students to repeat the case in the next class or to hand in their case notes or Case Preparation Chart. Another option and a particularly useful one is to take a time-out and raise the issue in class: "Look, I have prepared for a long time for this class and I had hoped that you would also come prepared. My impression of what has gone on so far is that most of you are not ready to engage in a serious discussion. Am I correct? What is going on? Let's talk."

The pink (yellow, green, red, blue, etc.) card option is offered by some instructors who recognize that, particularly in large classes, not everyone who wishes to participate will get a chance to be recognized. Thus, every student in the class gets one, two, three or four times during a course the option of holding up the card and thereby earning the chance to be recognized. The colored card raiser has precedence over all participants without a card. At the beginning of the course the instructor explains the rules and limits on the use of the card and from then on it is up to the individual student to decide when and whether to exercise the option. The colored card does give hesitant participators a chance to speak when they are most confident of the quality of their contribution.

Overactive Participation. Just as it is possible to have underactive participants, it is possible to have overactive participants. It is normally much easier to deal with the latter than the former.

The verbose students will get on the nerves of the class and frequently the class itself will control individuals like this and calm them down over time. Instructors may ignore hands that are outstretched and may invite certain individuals to come to the office to ask them to tone down a little. It is useful to point out to these individuals that every student has a responsibility and opportunity to participate and that, if they take too large a chunk of class time, others are automatically excluded.

Instructors use other means to manage a particularly active class, such as limiting everyone in the class to a maximum of one, two or three contributions.

Dysfunctional Participation. We refer here to empty, irrelevant, or out of place comments which may creep into the discussion. Again, each class should have some of its own discipline to handle such comments. When the instructor is trying to keep discussion to a certain point or certain area, it is proper to request that each participant concentrate on this area only. One may even ask, "Is it to this point that you're talking?" before allowing anyone to speak. If a point is relevant but out of sequence, it is easy to say, "Let's come back to that point later."

Dealing with dysfunctional participators nonetheless can be difficult. In the first place, the instructor should make it absolutely clear that rude and disparaging remarks and culturally or gender sensitive language are not tolerated. The first time a participant uses unacceptable language, the instructor should step in and remind the speaker and the class that such language is not to be used in this course.

As to other forms of dysfunctional participation, it is possible to discuss this directly with the student(s) involved outside of class.

Dealing With Material Related Problems

There are potential problems related to case materials that unsuspecting instructors should be aware of. These include: missing information and making assumptions, questions in class by participants, and case quality issues.

Missing Information and Making Assumptions. It is very difficult to find a perfect case. Thus, naturally, the participants will read and understand cases differently. They are forced to live with the reality that all desirable information may not be provided. It can then become habitual for students to come to class unprepared or frustrated because they think they did not have the necessary information. The instructors reply must be, "Why is the missing information so important to you, and how would it affect your decision? Secondly, what assumptions could you make that might be reasonable under the circumstances? And thirdly, would this information normally be available to the decision maker in this organization?"

Forecasts are a typical example. It is easy for participants to say, "The quality of this forecast is lousy, therefore, I cannot make any plans." It may well be very difficult to make good forecasts and good planning may have to allow for many contingencies.

Missing information and making assumptions are an integral part of the case method. In Chapter 3 in *Learning with Cases*, suggestions are made on how students can deal with missing information and making assumptions.

Missing information should actually be labeled: missing relevant information. By definition a case is but a part of a real life situation with lots of information missing. One possibility is that relevant information may be missing because the case writer could have inadvertently or deliberately left it out of the case. If it has been deliberately left out of the case, it may be at the request of the managers of the company from which the case was obtained or it may have been done for educational reasons. The other possibility is that the information was not available to the decision maker in real life either.

These are quite different sets of reasons. If the information was available to the decision maker in real life, but is not included in the case, the case writer could be asked to do a revision of the case. An alternative is to include the information as part of the assignment with the case, "Assume that last year's actual sales amounted to 750,000 units priced at $12 each." If the relevant information was deliberately excluded for educational purposes, the instructor may have to explain the reason in class, "The reason I did not give you last year's actual sales in units and average price was because I wanted you to use secondary data to estimate them and to show you how close you could come to the real number." If the data were not made available at the request of the organization where the case was written, an explanation can easily be given in class.

Should the data not have been available to the decision maker in the case, participants can be asked whether this is reasonable, whether the data might be obtainable, where it could be found, how much time and cost it would require to collect it, and how it would affect the analysis or decision in the case.

Arguments that missing information prevents a participant from doing a proper preparation is a popular one with participants who like to have any excuse for avoiding a decent individual preparation. A fact of life is that few decision makers ever have all of the facts they would like to have before making a decision. Therefore, making assumptions in case preparation and discussion is a normal and essential requirement.

Chapter 3 in *Learning with Cases* contains five types of assumptions which occur frequently. The context and "normal state of affairs" assumptions normally need little reinforcement with the group of participants who have collectively significant work experience. For groups without work experience they may not be so obvious. The decision criterion assumption, almost always needs to be made explicitly. If a class participant does not volunteer it on his or her own, the instructor will have to pull it out of him or her.

The "if-then" assumption, assuming that the alternative chosen will work perfectly, needs a fall-back position. "What would you do if your meeting with the president did not work out as planned?" is a standard counter question which can be raised by the instructor or a class participant. "Does everybody agree with this?" is a good way to elicit a class response to this kind of assumption. The "perfect person" assumption can be handled in a similar manner.

Assumptions can and should be challenged on the basis of their reasonableness given the case context and their relevance in view of the issue under consideration. Hidden assumptions, ones that are never explicitly stated, may prevent the suggestion or selection of alternatives for consideration and lead to an unsatisfactory solution. "I assumed this alternative was too expensive and, therefore, never suggested it," is one example of a potential hidden assumption. Both the instructor and the class need to make such hidden assumptions explicit.

Questions in Class by Participants. The case material can generate questions in the mind of the students. The instructor should not pass over questions that are pertinent. These are normally addressed by turning the question back to the student or classmates: "What do you think?" However, the teacher should not be led into wasting time with questions of little interest for the class as a whole. Students are adept at wasting time in class. One of the favorite games is to ask questions to the instructor,

"In your opinion or in your experience...?" or "Can you tell us a little more about this organization?" It is easy to spend 10 to 20 minutes a class fielding questions of this sort, particularly on cases written by the instructor. Normally, these are delaying tactics by students anxious to keep the instructor talking instead of jumping in themselves. Instructors who give in regularly to this temptation may well find themselves short of time to do more important things in class.

On the other hand, it is possible the instructor may find him or herself in the position of having to say, "I don't know." Frankly, when using cases, the possibility that instructors do not know is substantially increased. The case method deals with a tremendous amount of institutional information. It is unreasonable to presume that an instructor would be fully knowledgeable with all aspects of every case. Insofar as such information might reasonably not be known by the teacher, an "I don't know" in class is totally legitimate. If, on the other hand, it reflects improper preparation on the part of the teacher, students may well question why the instructor is allowed to get away with improper preparation and why they are not. For instances of the first kind, the class can itself be relied on to provide the insight or the information.

Case Quality Issues. There is another type of difficulty with some cases, which might be termed "quality issues." The quality of the language, spelling, grammatical constructions may not be correct, frustrating readers and preventing them from doing a sound preparation. The language may be misleading, so that a segment of the class sees it one way, while others have a different interpretation. Dates, numbers, and other facts may be confusing or contradictory. In one part of the case, it says last year's sales were $5 million; in another, $9 million, for example. There may be a legitimate reason for some of these differences in facts. Actual company documents may contain mistakes. (This latter issue should not be confused with different opinions expressed by characters in the case; such differing opinions are always a fact of life.) Insofar as these problems are a result of improper case writing, class participants should be shielded from these as much as possible. The best place to catch them is at the time of material selection for a course. Avoid using cases like this. Any problems which arise during class need to be dealt with quickly by the instructor, "I had not realized this was a problem; let's resolve it right now. I will make every effort possible to ensure that others using this case in the future won't face the same problem."

After class the instructor then tries to communicate the problems to the case author. If such efforts are unsuccessful, and the instructor still wishes to use the case again, corrections can be noted on the assignment sheet or on a separate hand-out. Under no circumstances should instructors make any changes to cases not written by themselves.

Pushing for Decision and Implementation

One of the key goals of the case method is to train participants to make decisions; that is, find solutions to problems on the basis of their analysis. Since participants are frequently inclined to avoid making decisions, some special initiative on the part of the instructor may be required to push them from analysis to decisions and from there to action and implementation planning. Logically, decision making and action/implementation planning fall near the end of the class. They are, therefore, subject to the greatest danger of lack of time to treat them seriously. Most instructors set aside a certain amount of time to give students some practice in these very important phases.

Quite often, several alternatives have been raised during the course of the discussion. No single decision may have been reached by the end and no attempt made to come to a specific conclusion. The instructor's plan may be to leave the discussion open so that students will think further about the case and come to their own conclusions.

However, to facilitate a confrontation of views on an issue or to heighten students' commitment to their opinions, the instructor may force the class to make a decision by asking for a vote. Sometimes a vote at both the beginning and the end will show the effect of the discussion on the class.

One way of providing an action orientation to the class from its very beginning is achieved by using "backward chaining," that is, by asking for action first and then backing into the analysis which would support that course of action.

Managing Time and Sequence

Since only a limited amount of time is available for every class, it is particularly important to manage time well. The use of the Case Teaching Plan helps provide control over the flow of discussion (see Chapter 4). Still, the instructor has to exert judgment repeatedly as to whether to push the class to move on to the next topic or to explore further the one being discussed.

Managing time requires the right assignment and discussion questions, a sound board plan and a sense of discipline, both in getting the details, evidence, facts and descriptions sorted out from the opinions. It may require comments such as, "Jim, I understand this is an interesting issue, but lets set it aside for a moment because we're still on the description of the short term strategy. When we get to the long term strategy, we'll come back to you." This level of control in the class is seen as critical by instructors who prefer a highly directive style.

Less directive instructors argue that there is a cost to control. There is less spontaneity and provocativeness associated with the classroom session.

Every once in a while, a student will crack a case wide open at the beginning of the class with super analysis and a logical conclusion. It may appear that there is little need for further discussion given the extensive job done by the individual. Such a presentation may prove to be a springboard for a better discussion than would have occurred without it. However, once the class has been given an opportunity to discuss the presentation and once it is clear that no one can come up with better ideas, there may not be much need to have any further discussion. It is possible to discuss the case to death. Class discussion can reach the point of diminishing marginal returns just like individual preparation and small group discussion in the Three Stage Learning Process. Occasionally, when a class has done an excellent job of discussing all the relevant issues with a case, it is possible to finish class early.

Maintaining Order

There has to be a reasonable degree of class discipline. Not all participants can talk at the same time. People must listen to the speaker of the moment. Without order in the classroom, it is impossible to conduct a decent case discussion. The role of the instructor can be compared here to the role of an orchestra conductor. It includes turning up the volume on the quiet ones, and toning the class down so that all can hear, as well as discouraging side discussions which might create noise.

In some countries the noise level in class tends to be higher than elsewhere. There is a tendency to carry on side discussions, to snap fingers, to talk simultaneously and to emit sympathetic and unsympathetic noises. It can be fun, but there is a noise threshold beyond which reasonable case discussion cannot take place.

Dealing with Trade-offs

The number of tasks the instructor performs during a case discussion is large. The objectives are multiple and varied. An instructor is concerned not only with the list of tasks and problems already identified but also with all of the normal tasks and objectives of any teacher in any circumstance. Thus, it all adds up to a very complex task continually dealing with trade-offs during the discussion. The difficulty is that many of the tasks have conflicting aims. For example, any time taken by the instructor to speak has to be taken from the students' participative time. An instructor who uses a great deal of control for the sake of efficiency may take away from the student the responsibility for learning. An instructor who plays an active role in cutting off discussion and orchestrating discussion may not encourage the class to exercise its own discipline. An instructor who wishes to use up time to discuss theory in class may not permit the students sufficient time to do problem solving or decision making or implementation planning. The instructor must, therefore, know how to manage trade-offs. These trade-offs are far from simple and can only be resolved in a total program and course philosophy. It is reasonable to do certain things in one class because in a previous class other aspects have been highlighted.

Humor in Case Discussion

Humor is ever present in case discussion. Humor can originate with the instructor and can be planned or spontaneous. Humor can also originate with participants. Humor (of the appropriate type and culturally acceptable) can be extremely valuable as a tension reliever and mood setter to create a learning environment which combines seriousness and fun. Clearly, the instructor's sense and use of humor is an integral part of his or her personality and teaching style. Professor Jones used humor as part of his case instruction, "Blame the airline." Some instructors very carefully decide on the use of jokes, cartoons, funny stories or quotes as part of their teaching plan. Others depend on the spontaneity of the moment or the participants to provide the humorous component of case discussion. Every class will have participants who see the funny side of a situation, who can phrase comments humorously, or who can feel the need for a humorous insert at the appropriate time. Such participants are wonderful contributors to a positive, caring class atmosphere in which vigorous intellectual pursuit is leavened with a joyous mood.

On the other hand, inappropriate jokes and attempts to turn a serious discussion into a farce or to make light of significant consequences can hurt the class discussion. Therefore, humor's role in case teaching can be likened to the use of spices in cooking. The appropriate spice needs to be added in the right quantity at the right time.

CASE TEACHING STYLES

In highlighting case teaching styles in a separate section, we are not trying to convince anyone that one style is better or worse than another, nor that in certain circumstances a particular style is preferable. However, style is an important element in teaching with cases because it embodies the personality of the teacher as well as his or her perspective on how students should learn.

Every case teacher must decide on his or her own teaching style: "What role am I going to play in the teaching learning process and how am I going to execute that role? The instructor's perspective on how students should learn will shape the teaching style.

In a classic article[1] about teaching styles Professors Skinner and Dooley at the Harvard Business School claimed that instructors who believed that the student was solely responsible for his or her learning tended to be non-directive in the classroom and used a "facilitator" approach. On the other extreme they called "demonstrator" any directive instructor who believed he or she was responsible for all learning. Skinner and Dooley contended teachers fell between these extremes and suggested a series of middle ground options where to varying degrees instructors shared the responsibility for learning with the participants. Perhaps the term "partner" could be applied to the mid-point position between the two extremes of non-directiveness and directiveness.

Though instructors tend to adopt a dominant teaching style, they have and do exercise the option of moving from one style to another depending on the position of the case in the course, the case difficulty, the time available, the quality of students, the learning priorities, the instructor's familiarity with the case method and so on. For example, a teacher might employ a more directive approach early in the case course and move to a more non-directive mode towards the end of the course as students gain confidence and improve their subject matter understanding and

[1] Dooley, A.R., Skinner, C.W., "Casing Case Method Methods," Academy of Management Review, April 1977

participative capability. Even within one class an instructor might employ several styles.

A case teaching style spectrum is provided in Exhibit 5-3 showing the relation between the instructor's perspective on the responsibility for learning and the degree of directiveness employed in the classroom.

Exhibit 5-3
DIRECTIVENESS, TEACHING STYLE AND
RESPONSIBILITY FOR LEARNING

	Directiveness		
	Low	**Medium**	**High**
Teaching Style	Facilitator	Partner	Demonstrator
Responsibility for Learning	Student	Student and Instructor	Instructor

CONCLUSION

This chapter discussed a number of considerations related to case teaching and reviewed a variety of tasks and roles.

Fortunately, the process of case teaching becomes a natural one over time. If it had to stay a totally conscious one, it would drive teachers crazy. Each teacher would be continually asking, "Am I doing the right thing in the classroom right now?" versus trying to solve the issue at hand. How I perform as a teacher in the classroom has to be secondary to the questions, "Are we concentrating on the problem? Are we solving the issue?" Teachers who genuinely are student-focused and have a solid problem solving orientation, can only go so far wrong in managing the participative process. Instructors must keep quiet a reasonable amount of the time, let students talk, and create an environment in which students feel comfortable in. These requirements are fundamental to teaching with cases.

There is no one best way to teach with cases. Instructors complement each other. It would be very boring if all teachers followed identical routines and used the same teaching styles in the classroom. Then they would become teaching machines.

class evaluation

The class is over, but the instructor's task is not. The habit of a regular evaluation after each case class is an essential part of standard case teaching. Class evaluation has six components: (1) participant evaluation, (2) Case Teaching Plan review, (3) material evaluation, (4) personal evaluation, (5) class assessment and (6) teaching note review and revision. It is our experience that many instructors engage in some, but not all of these activities. The after-class evaluation need not be overly time-consuming, but the discipline to do so shortly after every class, is important.

PARTICIPANT EVALUATION

There are four key questions in participant evaluation: (1) What is class contribution? (2) Why is contribution to class discussion important? (3) When is it evaluated? (4) How do case teachers evaluate contribution assuming some form of recognition is given to class participation? Whether participation counts towards a course grade has already been raised in Chapter 3 on course planning. It should be noted, however, that experienced case instructors make a habit of evaluating class participation regardless of whether credit is granted. Their purpose is to ensure that all participants over the length of the workshop, seminar, course or program are involved in the learning process. By noting who is strong and who is weak allows them to deal with each person appropriately.

What Is Class Contribution?

Contribution to class can be case or process-focused. Case-focused or content contributions deal with the case information itself and the associated theories and concepts. These become evident in the participant's analysis, alternatives, decision criteria, decision, and action and implementation plan. This category captures the largest percentage of all student contributions. It is important to emphasize that just repeating case facts in a class is not a contribution. Case facts can only be used to substantiate an analysis or draw a conclusion. Similarly statements like, "I agree with what John has said," are not contributions unless additional arguments are offered.

Case-focused contributions have both a quality and a quantity component. In our experience, student contributions can be mapped on the contribution grid shown in Exhibit 6-1.

Exhibit 6-1
CONTRIBUTION GRID

Low quantity means students have participated less frequently than the instructor expects and high quantity, more frequently. Low quality ranges from minor brief comments having little substance to small parts of the analysis and some basic interpretative comments. High quality means significant value-added contributions that advance the understanding of the class and are referred to by other students.

Process-oriented contributions deal with the discussion process, its timing and direction. A participant might say, "I believe enough has been said about the analysis, let's move on to alternatives." Or the opposite, "I think we need to discuss this part more extensively." Or, "I have heard lots of comments that are in favor of this alternative, but I would like to hear from those who are opposed." By making process-focused contributions in class the student shares the instructor role in managing the participative process.

Why is Contribution to Class Discussion Important?

Every participant is expected to contribute to the class discussion. Contribution to class discussion is the equivalent of practice in the training of an athlete or player in a sport. Without practice athletes or players would not improve their skills. Moreover, every student, knowing that he or she will be expected to participate in class will take more care in preparation and pay greater attention during the small and large group discussions. While some students find contribution to case class discussions a problem, we encourage students to view class participation both as an ethical requirement as well as a valuable opportunity. Class participation is an ethical requirement because each student while learning from others also shares the responsibility to teach others. Just being a sponge and drinking in the wisdom of others is not fair. Moreover, class participation is an opportunity to develop skills in verbally presenting ideas, persuading colleagues, debating, arguing and exchanging ideas and judgments. The opportunity to learn by doing and by teaching others lies at the heart of using cases.

When Is Class Contribution Evaluated?

Most case instructors evaluate classroom contribution undisturbed in the quiet of their office as soon after the class as possible. Recording evaluation during the class stifles the flow of discussion, produces added anxiety for students, and distracts instructors from managing effective discussion and exchange. It is not a common practice to have a separate "grader" in the class assessing student comments.

How Is Contribution Evaluated?

Chapter 3 has already commented briefly on how participation is evaluated. In some schools counting participation in assessing student performance is not allowed. In other schools, some professors count contribution to class discussion only to move students to another grade level, for example, a C+ to a B-. Other professors have significant weightings, up to 100%, assigned to participation. Most instructors are between these extremes. There is considerable variation in the tools and techniques that case instructors use in making their judgments.

The following nine guidelines require consideration in assessing class contributions.

1. Set a Realistic Participation Weight. Each instructor has to determine a weight for student participation as a percentage of the total course grade. In a course in which only one or two cases are used, contribution to class discussions should have a low percentage weight in assessing student performance. The higher the number of case class discussions, the higher the weight associated with participation can be. Moreover, the number of students in the class determines the number of times students can be expected to contribute to class discussion in a meaningful way. Using a rule of thumb of 25-30 meaningful contributions in an 80 minute class, a class size of less than 30 means each student can expect to participate in every class. In a class of 60 or more, once in every second or third class would be a normal contribution expectation. The number of case classes and the number of students in the class can result in class contribution percentages as part of the total course grade ranging anywhere from 0% to 100%.

2. Get to Know the Students. Chapter 2 outlined a variety of tools and techniques that can be used to help instructors to get to know their students. It is typical for case method instructors to use the class list, seating plan and class photo to help them recall who contributed in particular classes. If contribution to class is to count in the course grade, students cannot be anonymous to instructors.

3. Develop a System. A scheme, a model or a systematic way of differentiating between student class contributions is a necessary prerequisite for assigning a participation grade. Some instructors use word descriptions such as poor, satisfactory, good and excellent. Some instructors use a 1, 2, 3 system. Others have an A, B, C, and D ranking and others develop their own code. Whatever the system, it should be simple enough to allow reasonable recall and judgment after class.

4. Communicate the System. If instructors are going to evaluate student contribution to case class discussions, students have a right to know what the system involves and the instructor has a duty to explain the system. At the beginning of the course or in the course syllabus it is appropriate for instructors to explain what they mean by contribution to class, why they think it is important and how they intend to grade participation and when.

5. Keep a Record. Instructor assessments of contributions to case class discussions should be recorded. Relying on one's memory is risky. Typically, instructors make a chart of student names down the vertical and case class sessions across the horizontal and they make their notations student-by-student, class-by-class. It is also possible to record participation on the class layout sheet or on copies of the class photo.

6. Be Consistent. Whatever the system used and whatever the routine employed in the beginning of the course, it should remain the same for the duration of the course.

7. Record Immediately After Every Class. Reserve some time immediately after each class to review and record the contributions of all participants. Seasoned case instructors typically set aside 10-15 minutes after every class to perform this work. It is not effective to record every second or third class.

8. Provide Interim Feedback. Students also have a right to know how well they are doing in contribution to class discussions before the course finishes. Just as with mid-term reports and exams, interim feedback on participation allows students the opportunity to make necessary adjustments. This feedback can be provided on an exception basis or be universal. The form of feedback may vary from an informal verbal comment to a participation grade on a grading form, to a formal letter. Chapter 7 offers further comments on providing feedback.

9. Counsel Students. Interim instructor evaluation of student participation may result in student frustration and anxiety. Most of the counseling with students when teaching with cases involves participation problems. Instructors need to provide time and be willing to talk with these students. Chapter 7 elaborates on counseling students.

Some professors go beyond these guidelines and incorporate a weight for student self-evaluation as well as an evaluation of their classmates. In self-assessment each student is asked to evaluate his or her own contribution for a specific percentage of the course grade. Experience shows that most students tend to be fair in their self-assessment and in line with the professor's evaluation. Students may similarly also assess their classmates.

A further variation of student peer evaluation is to ask each student in the class to nominate those classmates whom they feel contributed the most to their learning during the case class discussions. More often than not the top 10% of the vote getters from the student nominations are the same as the professor's top ranked contributors. As an added twist, a professor may send a personal letter to the students' top 10% acknowledging this peer recognition.

In circumstances where student self-assessment is used, it is important that all members of the class have a common understanding of what contribution to class discussion means and practice guidelines 2, 3, 5 and 7 above. Student self and peer evaluation of contribution to class should not take over from the focus on learning.

Obviously, no single standard exists for how to evaluate and grade class participation nor how to communicate the feedback. However if an instructor chooses to evaluate contribution to class, serious consideration should be given to these nine guidelines.

CASE TEACHING PLAN REVIEW

It is useful to review the Case Teaching Plan for a few minutes after each case class. Was the agenda the right one? Were the estimated times realistic? Was the participation plan sensible? Did the board plan work out? Adding notes to the Case Teaching Plan and retaining the Case Teaching Plan in the case teaching file provide valuable references for the future.

Agenda

The review of the agenda deals with the extent to which the agenda was covered. What additional items came up that could have been added to the agenda originally? Were all of the questions or main topic areas of the case discussed adequately? The instructor needs to determine whether rearranging the agenda items and the wording and sequence of case questions would produce better results.

Time Plan

The time plan review is clearly connected to the agenda review. Did the class go according to plan? Where were the largest time deviations and why did they occur? Was the original time plan unrealistic or did something happen in this class that disrupted the time plan? If the time plan was not followed, was it better the way it actually went or the way it was expected to go? Given that most instructors tend to be ambitious in their time plans and given that the participative process is difficult to control at best, time plan deviations are to be expected. In view of the learning objectives for the class and the course, it should be possible to review the time spent on the main agenda items afterwards and make a judgment whether the intended educational value was obtained for the time spent.

Participation Plan

The review of the participation plan will reveal how well the call list and volunteer preferences worked out. How many of the volunteer preferences actually participated? It may also allow for reflection on whether the split between call list and volunteers was appropriate at various stages of the class discussion. Might it have been better to call on participants or to ask for volunteers? Aside from this split, the number of participants to be called for each agenda item needs to be reviewed. Would it have been better to call on a different participant for a particular question? Would it have been better to let participants with industry knowledge or relevant experience get into the discussion earlier or later? Who did not get a chance to participate even though they were on the call list? The participation plan review provides important input for the next use of the case. Additionally, in a case course the participation plan in one class becomes part of the input for the participation plan for the next case to be discussed in the course.

Board Plan

The board plan review allows the instructor to reflect on how good the original board plan was and where deviations occurred. Was there enough space for criteria definition and was it in the right location? Similar questions can be asked for each segment of the board plan. Some instructors go to the back of the class after each case class to make a quick judgment whether the board was legible, logical and fit the visual image originally intended.

The review of the Case Teaching Plan is likely to identify substantial deviations in a number of areas. Perfect adherence to the Case Teaching Plan in every aspect is not the goal of the class because it may create a rigidity not desirable in good case teaching and learning. The review after class must also recognize that any deviations from plan may have occurred because the original plan was not the best one.

Even if the original plan was a good one, unforeseen events may have happened in class. For example, the majority of the class may have had significant trouble understanding the assigned reading which the instructor believed to be self-explanatory. Or, a participant who had not yet spoken up in class started to talk and slowly covered some relatively minor points, but the instructor wished to encourage him or her to the maximum extent possible. Or, a news item covered a key topic area in the course and all class participants wanted to talk about it. Or, a case exhibit needed a lot of explanation in class. Or, as the discussion progressed, it became clear that a theory covered earlier in the course was still not clear and needed to be reviewed. Or, a participant presented a novel alternative not identified in the teaching note.

Any of these kinds of occurrences may have made it difficult to cover the agenda, time, participation or board plans as intended. Part of the instructor's judgment at review time is whether these were events that could have been predicted and incorporated in the plan, since the class was a better one because of the deviations.

MATERIAL EVALUATION

Assessing the quality of the case after teaching it is no easy task. The first concern is, did the case meet its teaching/learning objectives?

The quality of student contributions to the discussion is also a good indicator of case quality. Were students excited about the issue(s)? Did they apply the concepts and tools in the course appropriately? Did students relate the case to other cases and/or other courses? Were the exchanges between students lively and informed and to the point?

The way the case was written also affects the quality of the class discussion. Were there gaps in the story line? Were the numbers correct? Were there contradictions in the facts as presented? Was the case sufficiently clear to allow students to prepare an adequate analysis? If the case was significantly deficient, should it be replaced or should the instructor contact the case author and offer suggested changes?

Obstacles to case quality assessment go beyond the case itself and specific student reactions. Students may not have been sufficiently prepared. Something may have happened in another class in another course. The prerequisite tools and concepts may not have been adequately introduced. The case was placed too early in the course. Students found the case difficult to analyze. The case assignment was not clear. The instructor did not execute the Case Teaching Plan effectively. In view of these types of obstacles, new cases should not be automatically discarded because of one bad first class.

One of our colleagues has an interesting way of determining the quality of a case. He says with each new case it takes him three iterations to determine whether the case has educational value. The first time through, he is just barely one step ahead of the students regarding understanding, analysis and appropriate decisions. Sometimes he does not really hear what they are saying because he is unconsciously processing his own views. The second time through, he is much less concerned about analysis because his focus now is on the fit of the case in the course sequence. He is now listening for student commentary that reinforces earlier class discussions or that can be reinforced again in subsequent classes. The third time through he knows that the case works and is placed appropriately in the course and now he can really focus on the discussion process: Who needs to contribute? Who is saying what? What is the emotional tone? Who is struggling and why? Who has experience the class needs to hear? It is after the third iteration that he can feel truly confident in teaching this case.

PERSONAL EVALUATION

One of the most difficult evaluations an instructor must wrestle with is the one of self-evaluation. "How good was my preparation?" "How good was my own performance in class?" It is so much easier, if things went wrong, to blame the materials or the students. It is another matter to be objective enough to be able to assess one's own role in relation to the total process. "How much of the time was I talking? How many topic areas did I introduce? How much of the discussion was directed at me, as opposed to others in the classroom? Did I have the feeling that getting comments out was like pulling teeth? Was my mood right for this class? In retrospect, would I conduct the class differently if I had a chance to do it over again? If I had to rank my performance on a scale from 1 to 10, where would I fall? Did I learn anything in this class?"

If we could ever learn to be totally honest with ourselves, answers to such questions might be reasonably objective. Without recognition that the teacher's performance is an important ingredient in evaluating total class performance, one may easily come to the wrong conclusions.

CLASS ASSESSMENT

The next step in the after-class review concerns itself with the quality of the class just taught and the implications of this class in the context of the course as a whole.

Most instructors can generally tell after a class is over whether or not the class was successful.

There are several signs that indicate a good class. High student interest, with lots of hands up and wide participation is one positive indicator. Students voicing different interpretations regarding the same case information is another. When the discussion amongst students continues after the class ends also suggests success.

We know an experienced case method instructor who uses five "ifs" in assessing the quality of a class: 1. "If" the students were interested enough to give case preparation a decent effort. 2. "If" the students were motivated and cared enough to be interested in contributing to the class discussion. 3. "If" the case issues and challenges were truly important, real and critical to the focal person and to the organization. 4. "If" there was an atmosphere of freedom in the class for students to fail, to take a risk, to experiment, and not be ashamed with their colleagues or with the instructor. 5. "If" there was an atmosphere of pleasure, of fun, of respectful involvement and of camaraderie and intellectual hospitality.

The class review may also have course implications. If the class did not cover some points as well as it should have, is there an opportunity for reinforcement in later classes? If certain theoretical concepts covered earlier in the course were still not fully understood, should earlier classes have been taught differently and can adjustments still be made in the remainder of the course?

THE TEACHING NOTE REVIEW AND REVISION

There is no better time to review the case teaching note than right after the class has been taught. Are changes required under any of the headings of the teaching note? (See teaching note discussion in Chapter 4.) At a minimum, instructors need to put the reviewed Case Teaching Plan in the teaching note file as input for the next time the case is taught. The Case Teaching Plan review may result in changes to the teaching note or influence future plans for this particular case or other classes.

For new cases, especially after the first class, substantial revisions to the teaching note may be required to fill gaps that have been exposed by the first class. For most instructors the teaching note grows with each teaching of the case and becomes a valuable record and document of the experimentation that has taken place with the case over time. Even the inclusion of notes like, "I don't think the class was as well prepared as it could have been because most students were busy preparing for an exam in another course" may affect the future use and timing of this case.

CONCLUSION

The cycle of case preparation, class teaching, after-class review repeats itself every time an educator teaches a case.

The after-class review starts with evaluation of class participation. The temptation to go no further is strong. Most teachers are short of time. Even the few minutes to review the Case Teaching Plan, the case, one's own contribution, the class, and the teaching note are often difficult to come by. Yet, these steps are essential to the continuous improvement of the case teacher. Making the after-class review a habit removes the discretionary decision aspect of "will I review or won't I?" thereby becoming an automatic reinforcer of self-improvement. The collection of after-class reviews for each course constitutes essential input to course planning and improved teaching performance.

feedback and counseling

Feedback and counseling are an integral part of the case teaching/learning process. The prime focus here will be on instructor feedback to students on their class participation and on counseling those who are experiencing difficulties in participation. Additional topics will include evaluating student performance on case exams and feedback from students to the instructor.

FEEDBACK ON CLASS CONTRIBUTION

Informal Feedback

Informal feedback on class contribution starts during the case discussion itself. Positive body language, supportive head nodding, appreciative murmurs, writing comments on the board or overhead in exactly the same words as the participant used and keeping other participants quiet, while giving the individual a chance to take the time necessary to explain ideas fully, are all forms of positive informal feedback in class.

Some instructors thank participants once they have finished speaking; others say, "This was a great start," or "Your comments were very helpful," or "Well done." Other instructors are wary of such evaluative comments in class, fearing the absence of them conveys the opposite meaning. Therefore, they prefer other participants in the class to indicate whether they agree or disagree with the comments made by one of their class members.

Unfortunately, most participants find it more difficult to praise star performers than to disagree with those who are less able. Thus, even the noise level in class may rise when a less able student chooses to participate. Lack of negative feedback from classmates can, therefore, be interpreted as neutral or positive. Willingness of peers to reinforce points and to elaborate on them is already a positive reinforcer.

During the summary or conclusion phase of the class, the instructor has the option to review the most significant contributions made and single out certain participants, much as an orchestra conductor may recognize the contribution of certain musicians to the rendering of a particular piece of music. Asking the individuals to stand up and take a bow is not the normal routine in case discussion, but, "Paula's quantitative analysis really got our discussion off to a great start," or "Peter's suggestion that a much less expensive alternative might be available put us on a totally different track" are typical ways in which an instructor can give positive feedback in class.

The time period right after class, while participants have not yet left the room, may present an opportunity to nod to a participant and say, "Good job" or something similar. Giving feedback can occur in the hallway outside the classroom, the coffee area, the lounge area, the cafeteria or any other student gathering place.

The office feedback session as opposed to the counseling session may be initiated by the teacher or the participant. Some instructors invite all class participants to drop by any time they wish. Others have sign-up sheets. Some even discourage such participant-initiated visits. These face-to-face sessions, when they do occur, provide a great opportunity for frank exchanges. A participant indicates the prime purpose of the visit is to receive an opinion from the teacher, "How well am I doing in participation in your class?" This question comes in a variety of phrasings and is offered with a great range of intonations. A common reply is, "How well do you think you are doing?" Throwing the ball back into the participant's court is a good tactic. It forces the casual student to do some serious thinking and also to reflect on taking responsibility for his or her own performance in class. Moreover, the instructor learns more about this person. Finally, agreement with the participant's own assessment will help shorten the interview and disagreement can be focused on specific aspects. Should any counseling be required, it can be done on the spot or left for another time.

Formal Feedback

Providing more formal feedback on student participation is also a common practice. Some instructors prepare a brief individual memo for each student in which they give a written summary of their impressions. Comments like: "Your participation shows interest and preparation for class" or "You probably have a good knowledge of the subject matter" or "You seem to have a little trouble getting to the point when you participate" are more helpful than just a grade.

Some instructors write a more extensive personal letter for each student that indicates judgments on the quality and quantity of participation. The letter also contains some advice on what students might consider doing with the feedback. The advice for the low quantity contributor can be, "While quantity is not everything, we need to have active and wide discussions to collect the wisdom of the group. I would like to see you be more active in our class discussions." The advice for the high quantity contributor might be, "While quantity is not everything, we need to have active and wide discussions to collect the wisdom of the group. You are contributing your share and I urge you to continue." For the low quality contributor the suggestions may be, "My advice is to take more time when you have the floor and make a coherent argument rather than a single point to help move the discussion to a higher level" or "When you choose to contribute, you add considerably to our discussions. I would just like to see you contribute more of the same." High quality statements include, "Your contributions are strong and add value to the class discussion. Keep up the good work" and "Your contributions are memorable and add considerable value to the class discussion. We will all benefit if you continue to offer your insights."

Combing both quantity and quality as in Exhibit 6-1 in Chapter 6 leads to the following feedback statements. The low quantity, low quality participator is told, "Speak more often and contribute better." The low quantity, high quality student is told, "Speak more often and keep quality up." The high quantity, low quality participant is told, "Your frequency is fine, but improve your quality." The high quantity, high quality student is told, "You are doing great, keep up the good work."

Some teachers just take the participation grades they awarded students after each session, add them up and rank the class. The list of grades is posted by student number and then when students come, or are asked to come to discuss their performance, the instructor provides additional feedback.

COUNSELING

Given the complexity of the case learning/teaching process, instructors often find themselves in a counseling role with students. Although students develop ways and means of coping with ambiguity, case-based-learning can generate particular frustrations and anxieties. The greatest counseling challenge deals with participation in the class discussion. Other challenges deal with dissatisfaction with the participant's small group and individual preparation (see Chapter 4, *Learning with Cases*).

Contribution to Class Discussion Counseling

Frequently, students who have difficulty with participation in case classes will seek out the instructor to discuss their problems.

Counseling sessions may not only benefit the student, but also the instructor. Valuable feedback may be obtained as to what is going on in class, whether small groups are working well, whether certain instructor mannerisms are disturbing to the students and whether the material is being fully understood. This kind of session may also help the participant by identifying individual problem areas and helping plan remedial action.

During the counseling sessions the instructor must first diagnose the nature and causes of student concerns and then pursue possible remedies. The basic point in participant counseling is that the teacher does not have all the answers. However, the teacher must have the right questions. The participant plays a key role in the diagnosis and eventual prescription of remedial action. The non or ineffective participation in class can be viewed as a typical quality problem in operations. When things do not work out as planned, the cause and effect or fishbone diagram provides a useful framework for analyzing the problem. Therefore, in Exhibit 7-1 we have constructed a comprehensive diagnostic guide to assist in identifying the prime causes for inadequate participation by an individual class member.

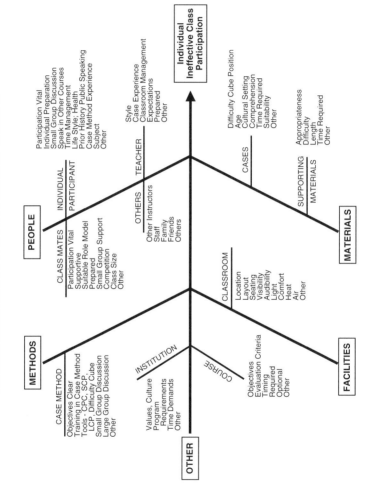

Exhibit 7-1
PARTICIPATION DIAGNOSTIC GUIDE

It will be useful to enlarge this guide to at least twice its size and to give a copy to the individual participant who needs counseling. The instructor must explain that on this guide are the most common causes for non-participation and invite the participant to record on the guide his or her own self-diagnosis so that it can be reviewed at a follow-up session. Starting with the physical facility is a neutral aspect to help put the individual at ease before moving to other areas. Most of the material on the bottom and left hand side of the guide is easier to address than the people category on the top right hand side. Involving the participant in the diagnostic and prescriptive process enhances the likelihood that remedial action will be effective.

Our experience is that most non-participators: (1) honestly do not believe that participation is that important; (2) have significant concerns or difficulties about speaking up in a large class and have a history of not speaking in public; (3) have course understanding deficiencies; (4) have difficulties in understanding the case method; and (5) spend too much or too little time in individual preparation. What is positive is that they recognize there is a problem when they come in for counseling.

The following pages will address these most common issues. The assumption will be made that the majority of instructors will be able to deal with most of the other items on the cause and effect diagram by themselves or with the aid of medical, psychological, or student counseling support.

1. The realization that class participation is vital. Ironically, participants who have done very well academically in educational programs or courses where memory played a significant role often find it difficult to adjust to the participatory requirements of case discussion. They are convinced that the final exam will reward their ability to memorize and often are not convinced that participation is vital to their success in a case course.

The parallel lies in sports. No athlete can become successful without practice. The would-be tennis player can watch the best players of the tennis world on television or videos and attend numerous lectures on tennis technique. However, sooner or later, the individual needs to hold a tennis racquet and to learn how to hit the ball. For the case method, the small group and the large group discussion are the practice sessions. Some instructors say the small group is the practice and the large group discussion is the game.

The key point is that the individual who knows he or she will not be playing the game or even participate in practice, and who will only be a spectator, will not be as motivated as the one who participates. It gets boring sitting in class and just listening to others. Lethargy sets in. Why read the case carefully when you know you are not going to be tested on it? Individual preparation slips. Small group attendance slips and participation is minor. The mind wanders in class, "The only reason I'm here is that attendance is required, but I am sure not learning very much." This attitude is a spiral to trouble.

Therefore, the first concern in counseling has to deal with the participant's recognition that class participation is not just for grades; it is the driver behind the learning process. Students should be directed to Chapter 5 in *Learning with Cases*. The participant who is ready to participate all the time prepares better, listens more actively to others, feels part of the process and accepts that he or she is responsible for learning. Truly, it cannot be emphasized enough, the case method requires a process of learning by doing and learning by teaching others.

2. Speaking up in a large class. A significant percentage of participants are not comfortable speaking up in a large group. Even those convinced of the vital nature of class participation find it difficult to face up to the implication, "You must speak up in class." Frequently, such participants make up their mind to participate in a particular class and then find they cannot. They return home and every successive failure lowers their self-esteem. This spiral is also dangerous. It is important to pull the individual out of it as soon as possible because the negative feelings spill over onto the course, the program, the institution and life in general.

Let us assume at this stage that the individual is at least comfortable with the course content and the decision model of the case method. Let us also assume that the individual does not need professional advice from a psychologist, psychiatrist or similarly trained counselor and is willing to work on remedial action with the course instructor and/or other teachers.

Identification of the fear of public speaking is the first step to recovery. The second step requires the will to do something about it. The participant's knowledge of self and preferences become particularly relevant. "Are you the kind of person that can motivate yourself or do you need other reinforcers?" is a good question to ask. "I am willing to help as are other instructors, but would you prefer it to be a classmate instead?" Here are some standard options that can be offered:

a) "You agree to make sure you will raise your hand at least once in each case class you have over the next week. You cannot control whether you will be recognized, but you can control whether your hand goes up. Make a record for a week whether your hand goes up and whether you were recognized and did speak in class. After one week come and see me. Let's set an appointment right now and we'll talk about how it went."

b. "I can arrange for myself and other instructors to call on you in class if you feel raising your hand is too tough right now."

c. "You may volunteer to start a class of mine or someone else's. At the start you can say exactly what you prepared without having to worry about what other people in class have said."

d. "You may volunteer for a presentation in my class or someone else's course."

e. "You may make a deal with a classmate, particularly someone who wants to participate more. Whoever participates more in a week wins a small reward from the other: some money, a drink, a snack, a movie or whatever. The point here is that a fellow student is watching you in class and you know it and you are doing the same for the other."

f. "You may just try to participate over the next week and then come back to see me. If it doesn't work we'll figure something else out."

The important points in these options above are:

- Let the participant decide on what he or she believes will work.

- Make the participant realize he or she now has an ally on the faculty who is willing and anxious to help.

- A process of improvement involving goals, small steps, and regular follow-up has started. Multiple office visits are usually required.

- The process of talking about the fears and feelings associated with public speaking allows the individual to face his or her challenge.

Our experience with hundreds of students is that the great majority find a way to cope and become reasonable participants. They are most grateful for the assistance and find all kinds of benefits beyond the passing of an individual course.

3. Lack of course understanding. It is entirely possible that participators do not wish to speak in class because they do not understand the course material. Therefore, to avoid personal embarrassment by a public display of their ignorance, they remain silent. Lack of course understanding should be comfortable territory for most instructors. The diagnostic process will require identification of where in the course difficulties arise and what the causes could be, including inadequate preparation.

Allowing individuals to provide a few hand-ins on specific topic areas to prove their understanding can help build their skills to the required level. Alternative readings or a tutor are other options.

4. The decision making model in the case method. A fairly high percentage of non-participators have difficulty with the process of analyzing and solving a case. They go through repeated readings and underlinings of the case but lack a logical process for the next steps. Such individuals often have difficulty even with the Short Cycle Process, the immediate/basic issue identification and the importance/urgency matrix. Referring students to Chapter 3 in *Learning with Cases* is often helpful.

5. Too much or too little time for individual preparation. Individual preparation time expectations form an important part of the teaching-learning contract between the instructor and his or her class participants. Whatever the time happens to be, for example, two hours for every class, it is vital to reinforce this expectation during counseling. Highly conscientious students whose previous superior academic experience was built on memory tend to slip into the bad habit of taking an excessive amount of time to read and prepare the case, (slow case reading is a particular challenge for foreign students). Thus, the student's life style changes too much. He or she spends most of his or her time studying while time for rest and sleep is reduced and time for fun disappears altogether.

The first improvement step for this type of student is to ask him or her to develop a weekly schedule that: (1) allows sufficient time for sleep; (2) includes sufficient time for "fun" activities of the type the student really prizes; and (3) schedules appropriate, but not excessive time for individual preparation and small group discussion. The student has to sleep well, eat well and have a well-balanced life before the problem of class participation can be realistically addressed.

The other extreme of the student who is unwilling or unable to spend enough time on individual preparation is normally not compounded by a general fear of public speaking. The student may have a part-time job or family responsibilities which prevent adequate individual preparation. Reducing the total course load may be the only option, if neither job or family time required can be lowered.

If the student is just lazy, then a reminder that inability to meet course requirements will result in course failure may be sufficient to motivate this individual.

Walking these participants through the Short and Long Cycle Processes as documented in *Learning with Cases* may be particularly helpful. Having them hand in Case Preparation Charts is a useful reinforcer. Reviewing opening paragraphs of cases and having them talk about the decision, the kind of analysis and criteria that might be appropriate, are also helpful. Often, such individuals are quite willing to spend the necessary time, but lack the tools.

A non-participator who comes in for counseling normally recognizes that he or she has a problem. The most potent counseling challenge of all is dealing with the participant who is afraid to speak in class, lacks some course understanding and does not understand the case analysis process. For this individual the solution begins with work on the course concepts and the case analysis process. Time will be a major concern because such a compound problem may not be solvable before the course is over.

CASE EXAMS

The two common written modes of evaluating student performance are case exams and case reports. In this chapter, the focus will be on how people use case exams. In Chapter 8, case reports are highlighted as a special variation in the use of cases.

For instructors using a significant number of cases in their courses, the use of case exams makes a lot of sense. Since case exams tend to "burn" cases, because so many written student analyses with grading comments on them will get out into the system, instructors may not be too anxious to use their best cases for exams. It is certainly good practice not to use the same case for exams in consecutive semesters or years. Sometimes using a brand new case for an exam can be a good way of testing it out for future inclusion in the course.

Selecting an appropriate case for an exam is much like selecting a case for a course, "What are the learning (teaching) objectives with respect to the three dimensions of the Case Difficulty Cube that are achievable with a particular case?" It can sometimes be a challenge to find a case that tests exactly what the instructor is looking for and is doable in the exam time period. Ideally, a case exam should cover similar analytical and decision making issues, conceptual knowledge and information management challenges as those raised in earlier classes, and allow the students an opportunity to demonstrate what they have learned.

With case exams typical practice is to bring students to a common site; allow three to four hours; make it open-book; provide a copy of the case and the assignment to each student; and collect the student answers at the end of the exam period. Students using computers normally turn in their disk containing the case analysis.

Grading Exams

We believe that acceptable performance on an examination must:

1. Identify and analyze the significant issues in the case.
2. Demonstrate an understanding of the conceptual and theoretical materials applicable to the case.
3. Identify the key assumptions, recognizing that different and sound assumptions will be made by different people on the basis of the same case information.
4. Demonstrate that the correct method was used when any analytical tool was applied. Since all exams will be open-book, obtaining a partially or completely correct answer will increase the grade accordingly.
5. Demonstrate that arguments used to accept or reject any alternate solution are consistent with the assumptions and calculations made, and are

consistent with the prior interpretations of case information.

6. Show consistency between the analysis performed and the decision recommended.

The decision to use cases for exams is a significant one. Grading of case exams is time-consuming compared to some other examination options. It may take anywhere from 20 - 40 minutes per paper, on the average, assuming a 2 - 4 hour examination period. Despite serious efforts to develop evaluation schemes, much of the grading is still subjective. Thus, there may be a significant gap in perception between what the instructor reads and what the student thinks he or she said. In view of this, it is no wonder that some instructors prefer to use someone else to grade the exam. Most case instructors prefer to grade their own exams because it gives them direct feedback on how well they have taught the course and how well students have learned.

Grading schemes for case exams vary depending on the case as well as the instructor. Some instructors have developed detailed grading sheets with grades assigned for every single point made. Others use blocks of marks for parts of the exam: 35% for analysis, 45% for alternative analysis and decision criteria and 20% for recommendations and a specific action and implementation plan. Still others have even broader schemes: "Does this student make sense?" If the answer is yes, the only thing which needs to be determined is how good the exam really is. If the answer is no, no amount of individual point totaling will make the whole an acceptable exam.

If case examinations are to be handed back to students, then every effort should be made to do so quickly. Ideally, it should be obvious from the reading of the comments on the paper why a student received a particular grade.

Sometimes, instructors may wish to schedule a special class session to discuss the case and its grading, and hand back the exam at the end of such a session. If the time gap between writing and return is too great, most students will have forgotten the contents of the case, making explanatory comments more difficult without their re-reading the case. Complaints are then almost totally grade-centered, without any reference to content.

In Chapter 6 in *Learning with Cases*, various types of exams and student instructions for them are discussed. Exhibit 7-2 provides a typical written case exam outline and Exhibit 7-3 provides a list of typical case exam evaluation criteria. The weighting decided upon by the instructor for each of the six categories identified in Exhibit 7-2 may be shared with the class before the exam. Both of these exhibits tie logically into the Case Preparation Chart. We have found that for very short exams the Case Preparation Chart itself can be used as the hand-in. Even in longer exams students often hand in their Case Preparation Chart in addition to the exam itself.

Written Case Analysis Counseling

Sometimes students are not satisfied with the feedback they receive on written work. Each instructor has a way of handling irate or disappointed students. For some it is as simple as, "Tough! Try harder next time." For others it is, "Let's sit down and take a good look at this."

It is good practice not to see a student for 48 hours after returning an exam. The student needs to get over the emotional upset. Students who want to discuss the exam have to re-submit their exam in advance with a one-page description of what they want to talk about and why. This procedure performs two functions. One, it re-acquaints the instructor with the paper to be as up-to-date with it as the student is. Second, the instructor knows what the student is upset about. Thus, the student hands in the paper with an explanation and makes an appointment. If the instructor finds him or herself in error, the instructor changes the grade.

Exhibit 7-2
TYPICAL CASE EXAM OUTLINE
(May vary depending on the case,
the course, and the instructor)

1. **Executive Summary**
   (Brief — one page summary of the main conclusions)

2. **Decision or Issue Definition**
   (Key decisions or issues to be addressed)

3. **Analysis of the Decision or Issue(s)**
   (Importance/urgency, causes and effects, constraints/opportunities, quantitative and qualitative analysis)

4. **Alternatives/Analysis**
   (Alternatives identification, decision criteria, advantages, disadvantages)

5. **Recommendations**
   (Preferred alternative, predicted outcomes, action and implementation plan)

6. **Exhibits**

Exhibit 7-3
TYPICAL CASE EXAM EVALUATION CRITERIA
(May vary depending on the case,
the course, and the instructor)

1. **Identification of Issue(s)**

2. **Issue Analysis**
   • Immediate/Basic
   • Importance/Urgency
   • Causes/Effects
   • Constraints/Opportunities
   • Quantitative/Qualitative analysis

3. **Alternatives/Analysis**
   • Analysis of alternatives provided
   • Generation of other alternatives
   • Decision criteria

4. **Recommendations**
   • Legitimacy of chosen alternative
   • Reasonableness of predicted options
   • Feasibility of action/implementation plan

5. **Logic**
   • Congruence between analysis and
     recommendation(s)

6. **Presentation**
   • Quality of language
   • Appropriate use of exhibits
   • Organization of the exam.

COURSE EVALUATION
AND INSTRUCTOR FEEDBACK

Up to this point, the issues in this chapter have been presented almost exclusively from the instructor's point-of-view. Students, the other key stakeholders in the process, have an interest in evaluation and feedback as well.

Student feedback can be obtained in a random and informal manner. A time-out can be taken during a class or a session can be arranged to ask, "What's going on in the course? What are you learning? What frustrations do you have? What about the discussion process? Do you have any suggestions for changes?" These time-outs are also an opportunity for the instructor to raise issues with respect to the students and their performance. However, this informal gathering of feedback carries some risk. Some students may make negative comments about the content and conduct of the course. An instructor needs to be prepared to deal with this kind of negative feedback.

At most institutions and in most in-house programs, it is normal to have a formal procedure for students to evaluate seminars, workshops, courses and instructors at the end of the course. Every institution has its own rating forms and procedures for retrieving and using this kind of data. It is one area in which standardization has not advanced very much. Nonetheless, such feedback can form a valuable insight into course planning and execution. Considerable controversy remains as to whether good teaching ratings and effective learning go hand-in-hand. One professor, after receiving a devastating feedback, commented, "My students still learned even though they rated me negatively."

Sometimes, especially in executive programs, participants are asked to rate an instructor and his or her materials after every session. There is a danger in changing the student role into an evaluator one and incessant instructor evaluation can change student learning to evaluation.

Whatever the merits of teaching rating systems, they can be used so that both students and faculty will be able to make a number of judgments regarding a course and its instructor. A course/instructor rating form is included in Exhibit 7-4 as a sample applicable to courses using cases.

In addition to these faculty-wide, typically end-of-the-course surveys, some instructors design their own form and collect information for their own diagnostic purposes. They list all of the cases and the readings and provide a rating scale. They ask about the equity of the evaluation scheme and the quality of the class discussion process. They solicit suggestions on the favorite parts, least favorite parts, and improvements needed of the course. Some instructors tell students when the course starts that they will solicit feedback at the end of the course and that students might want to jot notes on the cases and readings as they are discussed during the course.

CONCLUSION

Feedback and counseling when using cases is, undoubtedly, a challenge. In almost every area of the process, the questions are easier to ask than to answer. In this chapter an attempt was made to provide ideas and personal aids in meeting the feedback and counseling challenge.

Exhibit 7–4

Professor and Course Evaluation Questionnaire

Please mark the appropriate response to each of the following questions

On a scale from 1 (POOR) to 5 (EXCELLENT) how would you rate the following aspects of the course and professor

	1	2	3	4	5
1. The course overall?	☐	☐	☐	☐	☐
2. The professor overall?	☐	☐	☐	☐	☐
3. How clearly the professor communicated the learning objectives for the course?	☐	☐	☐	☐	☐
4. How successfully the course achieved the stated learning objectives?	☐	☐	☐	☐	☐
5. The contribution that cases used in the course made to your learning? (if the question is not applicable leave the response blank)	☐	☐	☐	☐	☐
6. The contribution that the textbook and other readings assigned for the course made to your learning? (If the question is not applicable leave the response blank)	☐	☐	☐	☐	☐
7. The contribution that projects, reports and other assignments used in the course to your learning? (if the question is not applicable leave the response blank)	☐	☐	☐	☐	☐
8. The contribution that other learning devices (e.g. simulations, videos, exercises, guest speakers) used in the course made to your learning? (If the question is not applicable leave the response blank)	☐	☐	☐	☐	☐
9. The effectiveness of the professor in utilizing the diverse perspectives and experiences of the students in the class?	☐	☐	☐	☐	☐
10. The effectiveness of the professor in providing timely and useful feedback?	☐	☐	☐	☐	☐
11. The assistance the professor provided outside of class?	☐	☐	☐	☐	☐
12. The effectiveness of the professor as a lecturer?	☐	☐	☐	☐	☐
13. The effectiveness of the professor in facilitating classroom discussions?	☐	☐	☐	☐	☐
	☐	☐	☐	☐	☐

On a scale from 1 (VERY LIGHT) to 5 (VERY HEAVY):

	1	2	3	4	5
14. Relative to other courses at the Ivey Business School, what was the overall workload for this course?	☐	☐	☐	☐	☐
	☐	☐	☐	☐	☐

On a scale from 1 (NOT AT ALL) to 5 (A GREAT DEAL):

	1	2	3	4	5
15. Relative to other courses at the Ivey Business School, how much has this course contributed to your development?	☐	☐	☐	☐	☐
	☐	☐	☐	☐	☐
	☐	☐	☐	☐	☐

SCANTRON FORM NO. F-5011-STC-L

case use variations

The focus to this point has been on the standard practice of teaching with cases. Both the participants and the instructor have come to the classroom prepared to discuss the case face-to-face. It is occasionally desirable to utilize variations around this standard practice.

The most obvious reason for using cases differently is a better fit with the learning objectives. Often, a particular variation provides a change of pace to relieve the case-after-case routine. Also, a particular variation is sometimes appropriate when only a few cases are used in a course.

The following variations around the standard theme are presented in this chapter: case presentations, case reports, role plays, case format variations, visitors to class, team teaching, and field trips.

For the first three variations, we describe what they are; why these variations might be selected; how to implement them effectively; and note some limitations and experiences for each.

CASE PRESENTATIONS

Description

Case presentations involve the live delivery of a prepared statement by one or more students to one or more people. Normally, case presentations are made by one or more small groups to the remaining members of the class and the instructor. Chapter 6 in *Learning with Cases* describes different types of case presentations and suggestions for presenters and critic observers. Case presentations offer a variety of permutations and combinations (see Exhibit 8-1). Each instructor needs to decide which option makes more sense given his or her course objectives.

Exhibit 8-1
CASE PRESENTATION OPTION LIST

- presentation format: *case competition, consultant, debate or town hall meeting*
- post presentation format: *regular class, question and answer, lecture, theory discussion or none*
- number of presentations per class: *one or more*
- size of the presenting group: *two or more*
- number of presenters in the group: *one or more*
- students: *assigned/volunteered*
- presenting group: *assigned/not assigned a point of view*
- time for presentation: *short/long*
- presentation notes: *handed/not handed in*
- grades: *assigned/not assigned*
- evaluation guide: *used/not used*
- non-presenting members of the class: *assigned/not assigned a role*
- critique group: *size and number*
- frequency in the course: *occasionally/often*
- presentation: *debriefed/not debriefed*
- debrief timing: *immediately following presentation/ later*
- record: *use video/not use video*
- presentation: *to class/specific person or group*
- format: *formal/ informal*

Purpose

Case presentations provide an opportunity for students to deliver a professional rendition of their case analysis and recommendations. Case presentations are also popular because they add variety to the class routine. Whether instructors use predominantly lectures or case class discussions, there are a number of reasons why presentations provide an effective option (see Exhibit 8-2). Most of these purposes can be achieved simultaneously.

Exhibit 8-2
CASE PRESENTATION PURPOSES

- add variety
- develop presentation skills
- develop communication skills
- experience making briefings to senior management
- emphasize action and implementation planning
- develop prioritizing skills
- develop time management skills
- practice using audio/visual supports
- increase the quality of preparation for a portion of the class.
- allow participants to teach each other
- force participants to prepare
- practice group dynamics
- develop listening and evaluation skills in non-presenting participants
- evaluate new case material

Implementation

Instructors can be helpful in directing participant attention to particular aspects in their preparation for the case presentation. Participants will have to deal carefully with information management, priority assessment and the art of presentation within time constraints. Following each group member's individual preparation, a substantial amount of time will have to be spent together in the small group to reach consensus on content and how to present the group's conclusions most effectively. Often, more than one small group meeting is necessary and, in addition, one or more rehearsals can be valuable. The Case Preparation Chart provides a good outline for the completeness of the coverage in the presentation. The emphasis will normally be on the preferred alternative and its implementation.

Limitations

Case presentations have their limitations. A major concern lies with the general lack of preparation from the non-presenting members of the class and their passivity during the presentation. There is limited group learning in the third stage of the learning process and the quality of whatever learning transpires in the class rests heavily with the quality of the presenting group(s). Generally the emphasis in oral presentation shifts to communication skills development versus rigorous analysis. Presenting groups spend a significant amount of preparation time in rehearsal and the development of visual supports. The equity principle says that every member of the class should get a chance to present. Invoking this principle heightens the above limitations. Also, a steady diet of case presentations becomes stale quickly.

Experiences

For many years, the management communications teaching group at our school has used case presentations involving all students as a standard part of their required first year communications course. Some presentations are for practice, some for grades, some for taping and debriefing, and some for a debate format.

One of our colleagues uses a very structured approach for presentations in her personnel course. She uses cases only at the end of various modules in the course and divides the class first into small groups and then assigns groups to either "analyst" or "critic" roles. On the "case" days she selects two analyst groups to present the case and two critic groups to appraise the presentation, while the rest of the class members assume the role of board of directors and/or stockholders of the firm. Following the analysts' presentations and questions from the board, the critic groups provide their feedback.

In some programs students engage in a three or four day, case competition format of oral presentation. Each small group prepares a presentation for each of three different cases. The case presentations are made by groups to judging panels of graduate students and faculty members simultaneously. Participating students feel some extra tension in this process and work through some of the stresses in group dynamics while gaining an opportunity to develop their presentation skills under friendly but competitive conditions.

CASE REPORTS

Description

Case reports are another commonly used variation in using cases. Here, participants either individually or in small groups submit a formal written statement of their analysis and recommendations of a particular case. Chapter 6 in *Learning with Cases* describes various types of case reports and preparation suggestions for students. As with case presentations, there are some options that instructors can choose from with respect to particular features of the case report (see Exhibit 8-3).

Exhibit 8-3
CASE REPORT OPTION LIST

- report: *individual/group*
- word limit: *yes/no*
- time limit: *short/long*
- assignment: *specific/not specific*
- format required: *formal/informal*
- suggested outline: *provided/not provided*
- executive summary: *required/not required*
- evaluation: *graded/not graded*
- grading criteria: *made known/not made known*
- graded: *by instructor/others*
- materials: *other sources required/not required*

Purpose

Case reports provide students the opportunity to do a thorough case analysis and to practice writing with clarity and impact. These objectives can be highlighted simultaneously with a range of other purposes as outlined in Exhibit 8-4.

Exhibit 8-4
WRITTEN REPORT PURPOSES

- promote rigorous case analysis
- practice preparing formal reports
- simulate the typical task force, team, project or consulting report
- practice using all dimensions of the Case Difficulty Cube
- assess performance
- practice time management skills
- use larger, more complex cases
- practice managing group dynamics
- practice preparing for case exams
- test newly written cases

Implementation

Individual preparation will take significantly longer for a case report than for a standard class discussion. In addition, if a small group discussion and common exhibit preparation are allowed, then several days of preparation may be expected. The Case Preparation Chart that results from both individual preparation and the small group discussion can serve as an effective outline as well as contain the salient features of the content of the written report. The more thorough the point-by-point outline on the chart, the easier it is to write the final report. The grading of case reports is similar to the grading of case exams already discussed in Chapter 6. Feedback and counseling on case reports is similar to case exams as discussed in Chapter 7.

Limitations

There are some limitations and concerns when using cases for reports. Perhaps the most obvious one is the time required for students to prepare the report and for the instructor to read, evaluate and provide feedback (also discussed in Chapter 7). There are other limitations as follows:

- Participants may plagiarize and hire ghost writers.
- Participant time spent on the report may negatively impact preparation for other courses.
- Participants may try to contact managers in the organizations where the case was written
- Collections of case reports may build, especially in student residences.
- Cases used for reports may be "burned" and not usable in regular class discussions for a few years.

Experiences

In some institutions the responsibility for a management communications program, including the writing of case reports, is assigned to a special faculty group. In others, individual teachers may choose to make a written case report part of their own course design. It is not unusual to assign two grades to a report, one for content and the other for presentation. In those institutions where case report writing is a formal program requirement, extensive manuals have been developed to explain expectations, presentation format, word limits and so on.

The distinguishing features of a case report, as opposed to a case class discussion or an exam, are the rigorous case analysis and attention to the written presentation. As some people have said, "Reports are power tests. Exams are speed tests."

ROLE PLAYS

Description

The typical role play asks the participant to take on the persona of a case character and to respond as one might expect this case character would respond. Trying to "be like" a case character in a role play is quite different from the standard case analysis and discussion process where participants are asked to step into the position of the case character but to bring their own personality and experience to bear on their interpretation of the data and the events contained in the case. As with the oral and written presentation variations, role plays offer a number of options (see Exhibit 8-5).

Purpose

Role plays can help to bring a greater emotional quality to the standard case class discussion. Participants become more committed to case characters and to the case events. Other reasons for using role plays are listed in Exhibit 8-6 and many of these can be achieved simultaneously.

Exhibit 8-5
ROLE PLAY OPTION LIST

- role play: *spontaneous/planned*
- specific format: *town hall meeting, debate, buyer/seller, negotiation, management/union bargaining*
- students assigned to role: *singly, in small groups, in sections, all to a role*
- scripts: *prepared by instructor/students*
- selection: *students selected/volunteers*
- following the role play: *debrief/not debrief*
- duration: *short/long*
- evaluation: *role play graded/not graded*
- context: *in class/outside of class*
- instructor: *involved in role play/not involved*

Exhibit 8-6
ROLE PLAY PURPOSES

- add variety to standard discussion class
- develop communication and listening skills
- develop negotiation, interpersonal, persuasion, and implementation skills
- practice dealing with consequences of actions
- make case analysis and recommendations more personal
- provide enjoyment in learning
- generate additional ideas and insights

Implementation

Role plays tend to be more successful if they are carefully planned. Instructors need to be clear why a role play should be used and which option should be the most appropriate to achieve the intended learning objective.

Limitations

Some cases are more conducive to role plays than others and some courses, such as organizational behavior and industrial relations, lend themselves better to role playing. There are potential challenges that instructors should note and plan for when thinking about role play possibilities.

- Role plays are difficult to execute well.
- Role plays can consume a lot of time.
- Participants in their roles can get off topic and away from the reality of the case.
- Role plays sometimes become a joke and are not taken seriously.
- Lack of information in the case leads to invention and fabrication of data.
- Role plays do not always work and hence need a recovery strategy.
- Sometime role plays can hurt people.
- Not all students make good role players.

Experiences

It is possible to use a debate style format in which different groups of students favor different alternatives and occupy separate sections of the class. The rest of the members of the class play a juding role.

Other cases, adaptable to group role playing, have been developed by instructors in industrial relations, with certain groups taking the union's side, others the management's position. Other cases present rich descriptions of various stakeholder groups involved in the issues and challenges, and the instructor has the option of separating the class into distinct interest groups, each pushing its point of view in a "town hall meeting" style.

A further variation on the spontaneous in-class role play is the use of incident cases to elicit participants' immediate responses. The incident process is a technique often used in human resources management training programs. Basically, the incidents are presented in very short, two and three paragraph, cases or presented by the instructor right in the class. For example, "You've just seen an employee strike a supervisor. What would you do?" Or, "One of your employees has just told you that she has been sexually assaulted. How would you respond?" Or, "Your boss emerges from his office in a stumbling, unsteady manner and makes his way towards the exit to the parking lot. The distinct smell of alcohol comes to your nostrils. What would you do, how and why?" These kind of incidents provide opportunity for participants to develop a broad range of interpersonal skills including conflict resolution, giving and receiving criticism, and counseling.

CASE FORMAT VARIATIONS

The three variations presented so far focus on the participant role and requirements. There are also some interesting variations in case presentation formats. On a continuum from the standard paper-based case at one end to the live case or field experience at the other end, we can identify three other variations. Cases can be presented in video, electronic and multimedia formats.

Video Cases

Video cases are the visual and audio equivalent of the words and data of paper cases. The term video case is not in the sense of a teaching aid, as reviewed in Chapter 4, but as a self-contained case that is used with or without a paper case supplement. When used by itself, a video case requires individual preparation during the video play itself and it is normal to stop the video periodically during the class to allow for further individual preparation, small group discussion and/or large group discussion.

One of the benefits of using a video case is that it reduces the preparation time. Each member of the class starts and finishes at the same time. There are also the added benefits of adding variety, more spontaneity in the class and better visual detail.

Video cases are in short supply because of their high cost and the added challenges involving release and disguise. Even if they are available, the analytical rigor, particularly quantitative work, may be less, especially when the video case is used by itself. As well, video cases tend to take more class time for both individual preparation and discussion.

Electronic Cases

In its simplest form, the electronic case format provides the paper case data on a computer disk. The paper-based case has been supplemented with spreadsheet software and electronically conveyed data for some time. Presenting case text, data, exhibits and graphics on a CD-ROM is a natural extension.

Electronic cases allow more data to be included along with a richer presentation format to capture student interest. In this regard, students get more practice in working with the presentation dimension of the Case

Difficulty Cube in terms of specifying relevant information.

An obvious limitation to the electronic case format is cost. Electronic cases may be expensive to produce. As well, there are costs associated with providing a physical and technical support structure.

Multimedia Cases

The multimedia case is a combination of both the video and the electronic case.

The obvious reason to use a multimedia case is that it comes closest to the real life situation. Multimedia cases can support and enhance the richness of paper-based cases.

However, producing a quality multimedia case can be expensive. The added costs for student hardware and technical support structure are the same as for the electronic case. Multimedia cases present even further limitations. With the increasing complexity of data and presentation modes, student preparation time expands. Release and disguise of information along with copyright infringements and obligations for both producers and users become more complicated with multimedia cases.

Use of Cases on the Internet

In long distance learning, small group or large group discussions that are part of the Three Stage Learning Process represent the major challenge of participative learning. Both the professor-student and student-to-student interfaces are different. Considerable experimentation is currently in progress in different parts of the world to find effective means of using cases on the Internet.

VISITORS TO CLASS

An interesting variation is to invite a visitor or visitors to attend the class. The visitor list can be quite broad as indicated by the following possibilities:

- the focal person in the case
- a representative from the organization in the case
- a person in a similar organization or in a similar industry
- an expert on the issue(s) addressed in the case
- the case writer
- a person from the same culture as represented in the case
- a person from a different culture as represented in the case
- a guest instructor who knows how to teach the case very well or who has some special knowledge
- a fellow teacher whose subject area is a significant aspect of the case

Inviting visitors to class can add substantially to the credibility and relevance of the discussion. It becomes easier for participants to see the connection between the class discussion and the case data and the real world. If the visitor happens to be an expert in the field, participants have an opportunity to learn just what it is that experts really do. It is useful to videotape a guest's contribution to the class and hence provide a more permanent record of the visit, just in case the guest is not available the next time the case is used. The videotape can be edited and added to the case teaching file.

Instructors need to plan carefully in order to obtain the educational value that visitors can add. It is common, for example, to have the visitor participate in the last third or quarter of the class as opposed to the beginning. Visitors may comment on the range and depth of the class discussion, field questions and outline the rest of the story, if the visitor is the focal person in the case. If the visitor is an expert with respect to the issues in the case, he or she will be able to discuss current practice. Visitors should be briefed before the class begins on the nature of the course, the characteristics of the participant group, the typical case discussion format, and the likelihood of hearing comments that the visitor may believe to be naive, erroneous and sometimes critical of company people or practices. Instructors will also have to decide whether to introduce the visitor to the class at the start versus the end of the class. If the introduction is at the start, it may reduce the spontaneity and range of the discussion. If the visitor's introduction is at the end, it may be perceived by the participants as deceptive and unfair.

The introduction dilemma is but one of the difficulties with visitors to class. Other limitations include the risks that the visitor becomes upset with some remarks made during the discussion, the visitor is ill-prepared and bores the students, or the visitor breaks the disguise of the case. In addition, this variation, like others presented earlier, takes time.

TEAM TEACHING

Certain cases lend themselves to team teaching; that is, two or more instructors jointly conducting the classroom discussion. This variation is used most often with multi-disciplinary or very complex cases.

Team teaching provides an opportunity to show the faculty as a team. Various faculty members can take on various roles, represent different functional areas, or focus on specific parts of the discussion. As an example, in one of our executive development programs, the four member faculty team all participate in the first introductory case discussion session. The participants get to see all the instructors early in the program and the faculty have an opportunity to demonstrate the consistency of the message and the seamless nature of the program focus on the decision making process.

Team teaching is obviously an expensive use of faculty resources. Although some instructors find it cumbersome and difficult to execute, those instructors who have tried it generally believe it is a useful device in class discussions. This case use variation requires that each member of the team has a reasonable amount of case teaching experience.

FIELD TRIPS

Field trips provide a wonderful opportunity to reinforce classroom learning. Sometimes the trip is to the company represented in a case and becomes a valuable supplement to the case. Sometimes the trip is to a company in the same industry represented in a case and here, the participants have a chance to see a similar process and talk about similar immediate issues and challenges. The trip to a company in an industry not represented in any case in the course can be turned into a live case if company managers are willing to talk about specific challenges.

Instructors often require students to complete a field trip assignment. In particular with our Executive MBA Program, one of our colleagues schedules the trip to follow the first three or four sessions of the course. He tries, as well, to arrange this trip to the facility of one of the participants in the class and this gives the group an instant welcome while providing the hosting participant a chance to show off his or her company. The instructor requires each participant to write and hand in to him, what he calls a "Dear Boss Memorandum." In this 800 word memorandum addressed to the participant's actual boss, he asks students to comment on three questions: (1) What was seen and heard? (2) What were the key learnings; and (3) Based on what was seen and learned, what should the student's company do that it is not currently doing or what is it doing that should be maintained and emphasized? The feedback he gets from the participants is generally the following, "Good exercise, I've already sent this memo to my boss."

For full-time students the field trip assignment may relate to topic areas already covered in the course and ask for the participants' comments.

Field trips, like other variations, take more time and incur some financial cost. The added limitations here include getting access to a company and making the administrative arrangements, managing generally large numbers of students during the visit, and dealing with concerns for safety, confidentiality and liability.

CONCLUSION

Variation within any routine can provide a welcome change of pace. Even with the excitement that cases can create, a steady diet of routine case discussions can be tiresome. As outlined in this chapter, there are many variations available to choose from. Some focus on what students may be asked to do differently; some on what instructors can do differently. Others involve technical and multimedia variations in case formats.

The most compelling reason for varying the standard case approach or format is to achieve the teaching/learning objective better.

special considerations

It is almost inevitable that a number of interesting topics related to teaching with cases would receive insufficient coverage as a result of the topic outline chosen. It is, therefore, useful to have a chapter which can pay attention to these points. They will be addressed under four main headings: (1) teacher training will cover various ways and methods to train new instructors; (2) diversity will survey situations where students, instructors or materials are not homogeneous; (3) student shortcuts and cheating, although an unsavory subject, will provide some insights as to how instructors might deal with such behavior; and (4) case use in a non-case environment.

TEACHER TRAINING

It may appear somewhat strange to treat the topic of teacher training as a special consideration, since the key purpose of this book is to help in the development of case teachers. Nevertheless, it is useful to address in a separate section what can be done about difficulties faced by instructors new to the use of cases.

New professors often come straight out of their doctoral program with a strong theoretical but weak application background. Teaching with cases may induce anxiety because they do not feel they have the same control as when lecturing. Teaching with cases requires self-confidence and tolerance for ambiguity. Instructors have to be able to think on their feet and react spontaneously. In addition to thorough familiarity with the course content or subject matter, case teaching requires proficiency in the teaching - learning process.

Although it has been said that teachers are born, not taught, we believe that it is possible to help instructors new to teaching with cases become competent and proficient faster.

Orientation Efforts

Instructors new to the use of cases need to learn the norms and processes of their institution. Often this is done informally. At the beginning of each academic year many large schools offer an orientation session for new faculty. Presentations are given on the school, its various programs and research activities, as well as its case teaching philosophy and expectations.

Taking a Case Course

Another option for new faculty is to sit in on a case course as an observer to see what the instructor is doing and how the students are reacting. The benefits of this exposure will increase significantly if the new instructor has the opportunity to debrief after each class with the seasoned teacher or faculty team.

Teaching Files

Without negating the necessity to prepare one's own teaching notes for each case to be taught, as discussed in Chapter 4, sometimes extensive teaching files exist that include the teaching notes of various teachers for the same case. These files represent the cumulative experience of teaching that one case and may prove quite useful to the unseasoned instructor.

Teaching Planning Sessions

In multi-section courses using cases, all of the faculty teaching the same course may meet regularly to plan how they will teach each session in the course. The benefits of such teaching groups in preparing for a case parallel those of the small group discussion for students, as described in Chapter 4 of *Learning with Cases*. Such teaching meetings augment what is available in the teaching notes and new instructors find them helpful.

These meetings may include a general discussion on the course and the fit of the cases. Discussion may cover educational objectives to pursue and strategies to reach these objectives. Most of the discussion will focus on individual cases, possibly concentrating on difficult analytical or conceptual issues. More experienced instructors may identify potential pitfalls and suggest possible ways of handling them. The group may take 30 to 60 minutes per case, depending on its complexity. If necessary, it is possible for a new instructor to pursue the discussion with a more seasoned teacher after the group meeting.

Visiting Classes

Visiting classes can take two forms: the new instructor visits the class of another teacher or invites another teacher to sit in his or her class.

Sitting in another teacher's class requires that the new instructor has at least prepared the case. Visiting should be done with the permission of the teacher, and may or may not involve a debriefing session afterwards. Most faculty are receptive to providing this type of assistance. If visiting classes is done extensively with a number of colleagues, it will provide exposure to a variety of teaching styles and approaches. It may also encourage and assist in the development of one's own style.

A more traditional type of visiting involves the experienced teacher visiting the novice instructor's class. While some senior faculty make excellent coaches, not every one will be skilled at pointing out deficiencies and providing pertinent feedback or suggestions, beyond some obvious pointers such as, "Try to avoid speaking only to the right side of the class." Not every junior instructor is receptive to criticism either. It may just be that the respective teaching styles are not compatible.

Videotaping

Having a videotape made of a class can be a useful but humbling experience. The camera does not lie. All dysfunctional idiosyncracies and mannerisms will be revealed. The benefits come not only from seeing but also hearing oneself. Reviewing the video can be done alone or with the assistance of an experienced instructor.

Case Teaching Workshop

Having taught case teaching workshops for more than 30 years all over the world to over 8000 participants, we believe that the basics of good case teaching can be taught in a workshop setting. We also believe that experience is a great teacher. Every instructor has to decide on his or her own which case teaching approach is most effective for his or her students, course, and own personality. Knowledge and understanding of the prerequisites, the preparation task, the case teaching process, evaluation and case use variations permit the new instructor to build on the insights and experience of others. By avoiding the most obvious mistakes and speeding up his or her learning curve, the new instructor can become effective and enjoy the case teaching experience faster.

DIVERSITY

Managing diversity is important for those trying to teach with cases. Three aspects specifically addressed here include: (1) students with a different cultural background; (2) instructors with a diverse background; (3) and cases with a different cultural background.

Students with a Different Cultural Background

Many educational programs often attract substantial numbers of students from other countries. These students come from all kinds of backgrounds and bring diverse values to class.

In so far as different cultures also mean different educational values and norms -- for example, stressing rote learning, memory work and the ability to recall large numbers of facts -- cultural diversity may mean an extra challenge for the case teacher. It may be difficult to persuade some students to engage fully in the Three Stage Learning Process, including all of its team work and participative norms. It may also be difficult to dissuade some students with diverse backgrounds from trying to memorize cases instead of analyzing them and to learn from fellow students instead of the instructor.

Case method familiarization workshops have a high pay-off if they are well done. In such workshops students can reflect on the implications of the case method for themselves individually and collectively. Full understanding of the challenges presented by the case method has to be an integral part of such familiarization efforts. Many students have difficulty grasping the full implications of the case method with respect to their norms, values and behavior.

The teacher's own behavior must be a living example of what he or she is asking the students to do. Each instructor must demonstrate respect and tolerance for the variety of views and values expressed in class. Such modeling on the part of the instructor will be instrumental in students' learning to value diversity, be it cultural or intellectual.

Instructors with a Diverse Background

Case instructors are often invited to give seminars, to teach in executive programs or to assist in developing management programs elsewhere. Also, students go back to their respective countries and start teaching there with cases. Both types of instructors share the problem of adjusting themselves and their teaching to different cultural environments. The viewpoint of the visiting teachers will be emphasized here, assuming that the second type of instructor will find it easier to deal with the cultural issues involved.

The ideal would be for the teacher to be not only completely culturally attuned, but also to be able to speak the local language. Simultaneous interpretation, however, is expensive, adds a significant barrier to spontaneity in case discussions, and lengthens the time required. Increasingly, it has been our experience with the advent of globalization that many participants are able to function in English and will often assist classmates who are less fluent.

In any event, the instructor should speak slowly, avoid idiomatic expressions and jargon, repeat himself or herself frequently, and, if possible, try to alter his or her behavior to conform with cultural norms.

At the very least, the instructor must be aware of his or her own cultural biases. The instructor must also be open to different behaviors on the part of students, different interpretations of case facts, and different approaches to solving cases. And finally, as much as possible, case materials must be selected taking in consideration the culture where they will be taught.

Cases with a Different Cultural Background

All cases are culture bound. A large amount of information is frequently not included in a case although many case teachers may not be overly sensitive to this fact. The missing information is assumed to be standard cultural, historical and societal knowledge that any student should know through normal upbringing. Thus, when we say an organization is located in Los Angeles, at a specific time, it is assumed that no further explanation is required regarding the city, or the economic or other conditions prevailing at that time and place. How startling a difference time and location can make is obvious when the same case is set in London, Moscow or Hong Kong. A lot of relevant information is actually not included in the case. It is presumed to exist in the reader's mind. When an instructor goes to a different country, it is not safe to assume that these non-explicit case data will be recognized in the new environment.

Sometimes, non-local cases can be used to increase student interest and to broaden their horizons. The percentage of non-local cases has to be considered carefully, though. Excessive dependence on such cases may well turn students off because they feel the material is not relevant to their own environment.

SHORTCUTS BY STUDENTS

Students may try to avoid all or some of the responsibilities associated with their learning with cases and seek "shortcuts." It is useful for the instructor to recognize the nature of possible shortcuts and to find ways and means of dealing with them. The range of severity in terms of ethical considerations may be substantial and will have actual cheating on one extreme. Most issues deal with the preparation of a case for class and, since this may be perceived as overly time-consuming by students, ways and means of avoiding the necessary time investment are the most popular form of shortcut.

Three ethical issues are: (1) giving, receiving or soliciting notes on cases before or after class; (2) contacting the case organization to find out what decision was taken; (3) avoiding preparation and depending on the small or large group discussion to reveal the salient learning points of the case.

Since the philosophy of learning with cases is based on the principle of growth through experience, the individual who is trying to bypass the system loses the most.

Moreover, if an instructor's note gets in the wrong hands, or if extensive student note files are kept in a fraternity, sorority, student residence, or passed on from year to year by students, the net effect will be that the cases themselves become useless. Having to give up a good case because of potentially widespread distribution of the "answers" is painful and costly. All instructors know good cases are difficult to find and "burned" or "blown" cases are sad victims of unfortunate circumstances.

Contacting the case organization to find out what decision was made should be strictly prohibited. First and foremost it could ruin future case writing collaboration. Second, it may lead the students to believe that the company took the right decision, which may not be true.

Shortcuts to Preparation

The most obvious shortcut is not to prepare for a class at all; no reading and no preparation. Some teachers tell students that they wish to be told of such a situation before class. Clearly, in case of emergency, lack of preparation is understandable. Most students do not believe it is in their best interest to tell the instructor before class, for fear of creating a bad impression. They prefer to take their chances in class, where the probability the instructor will find out appears to be low. Even when the instructor does ask such an unprepared student for a contribution, two options exist. One, the student may admit to not having read the case. Now it is up to the instructor to have a response ready. If the instructor has told the class, "Prior notice is required," he or she can say, "My norm is that I wish to be told before class." Some prefer to add, "Please see me after class." Others will say, "Don't let it happen again!" A few just move on to the next contributor.

The other option is for the student to try to bluff. On the basis of what discussion has already taken place, the student may be able to "grab a little piece and try to run with it "creating an awkward situation for both sides, if it is subsequently uncovered that the student does not know what he or she is talking about.

A step removed from total lack of case knowledge is the situation where the student reads the case, but does no analysis. Comments like: "I had trouble getting a handle on this case," "I did not understand the technology," "I did not understand how the system worked," are some typical warning signals in class. If the instructor takes such comments seriously, class time and effort may well be wasted. If situations such as these happen rarely, there is no great cause for instructor concern; although, if they are concentrated with certain individuals in class, action is clearly required.

Instructors accepting mediocre or no preparation on the part of one or several students will have to deal with the consequences. When class members believe that a student got away with no preparation or fooled the instructor into believing that it was a good preparation, they may develop bad habits. Other students may start believing that they can "work the system" consistently and get away with it. Instructors are therefore well advised to not accept on any regular basis students who fumble, ask irrelevant questions, regurgitate case facts, or talk a lot but say little. Instructors must convey the clear message that such behaviors are not acceptable. The message does not have to be passed in an angry or penalizing tone. It can be done using humor or simply reiterating the importance of good preparation.

Some students come to class with a minimum amount of preparation, if any, but are clever enough to pick up the drift of the discussion, and come on strong near the end of the class with discussion summarizing or repetitive comments. This type of shortcut may be called "on-line" preparation.

When a large segment of the class comes unprepared, it is a more serious situation. The instructor should stop the class and ask why this has happened. Students may have a good reason. Normally they do not deliberately try to avoid learning. There may have been an exam or a party the day before.

Sometimes students will prepare a certain percentage of cases well and others lightly. A special type of this shortcut is where study groups assign cases for preparation to certain individuals on the understanding that others may just read them. For example, in a group of six students working on three cases, each group of two students would do a "serious preparation" of one case and read over the other two cases. Then, in the small group discussion, every participant "gets clued in" to two cases, and "presents" one case. If certain group members have special skills or backgrounds, such as accounting, marketing, finance, operations, or others, this kind of arrangement is particularly appealing from a time efficiency standpoint. Letting the "experts" prepare the cases they are best equipped to handle may be tempting. Such practices may be difficult to uncover for an instructor who has no knowledge of what transpires in learning teams. It is obvious that the learning of the non-experts will be cut short by such arrangements. We do not consider this kind of preparation sharing a desirable practice.

Occasionally, students have a contribution strategy such as, preparing well near the beginning or end of the course, or doing especially careful preparation every fourth case, or some similar strategy.

Whenever an instructor suspects one or several individuals of not preparing properly, discussing concerns with the individual(s) outside of class is useful. If it appears that a large percentage of the class is not prepared, a "time-out" in class to discuss this impression is required.

When shortcuts by students are caused by excessive length of cases or accompanying reading assignments, the instructor may wish to review whether proper preparation was realistic given the "contract" between teacher and students regarding preparation time.

Seat Visibility

The student's seat selection in a room may indicate his or her preference for visibility or participation avoidance. The typical case classroom may be divided into areas of high visibility to both instructor and other participants and ones of lower impact. In tiered rooms with a semi-circular arrangement, the highest visibility area is in the center rows directly in front of the instructor while the lowest visibility zones are on the front sides. (See Exhibit 9-1.)

Exhibit 9-1
SEAT SELECTION

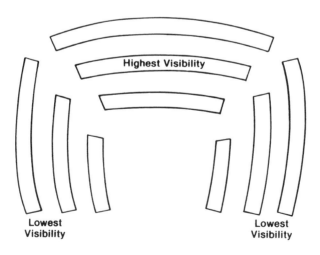

Group Projects

When groups work on projects together, which may or may not involve presentations in class, the work load may not be shared equally among students. Some instructors prefer to ignore this aspect and choose to give a common grade to all group members. Others ask group members to grade each other, possibly anonymously.

Exams

It is logical to use case exams on a course where a significant amount of the course is devoted to cases. Communication between students on exams, where such communication is not allowed, does constitute cheating, as on any other exam.

CASE USE IN A NON-CASE ENVIRONMENT

Teaching with cases in an environment where the use of cases is the exception presents some special challenges.

The three fundamental prerequisites: suitable physical facilities, getting to know students, and finding and distributing the case material tend to be magnified in a non-case environment (see Chapter 2.) Major additional challenges are changing student, faculty, and institutional perspectives on the case method.

Student Perspective

If only one instructor uses cases in an institution or program while other instructors use other teaching methods, participants will have to adjust significantly to the norms of case work. The habit of preparing for each case class rather than for exams is not an easy one to acquire. Learning to learn from each other (in addition to the instructor) and learning to teach one another are often new skills for most participants. Finding time and motivation for individual preparation and small group discussion outside of class may not be easy either. The instructor needs to be very clear, therefore, in explaining why cases are an integral part of the course, what benefits can be expected from using cases in the course, and how participants should do their part in each stage of the Three Stage Learning Process to maximize their learning.

Faculty and Institutional Perspectives

Faculty members may make disparaging remarks about the use of cases not only to case teachers and other faculty, but also to students. These comments create an unpleasant atmosphere at best and, at worst, work counter to the case teacher's purposes.

Faculty attitudes are often also reflected in institutional attitudes, values, rules, norms and processes. These may be roadblocks to effective case teaching and learning and may also affect promotion and tenure decisions.

In some schools and some programs there is no requirement and little encouragement for students even to attend class. In some locations it is simply not allowed to evaluate participation in classroom discussions for performance assessment purposes. Incentives to encourage instructors to devote time and energy to teaching with cases are often non-existent. There is no, or very little, training available in teaching and learning with cases. Instructors in such institutions not only have to convince themselves and their students but also their colleagues and, especially, their department chairs of the benefits of using cases.

Moreover, in terms of the reward system and promotion criteria, if the university sets itself up as a research institution, good teaching often is not recognized in tenure and promotion decisions. As a result there is little incentive or perceived legitimacy to engage in case teaching.

CONCLUSION

This chapter's four main topics, training of case teachers, managing diversity, shortcuts by students, and case use in a non-case environment, all represent challenges in teaching with cases. Teachers new to the use of cases can learn the basics of effective case teaching reasonably quickly, provided they go about it the right way. Case teaching workshops, augmented by readings and the assistance of experienced case teachers, have proven effective ways of improving teaching performance.

Diversity in students and instructors, discussed in a cultural sense in this chapter, also exists in gender, experience, age, education, and skill sets. The ability to recognize, understand and use diversity as a positive force in teaching with cases permits the instructor to impart to students skills which will allow them to manage globally. The diversity of cases presents an opportunity in course planning and classroom execution to reinforce almost all aspects of diversity management. The case instructor leads by example, a challenge that is easily forgotten and bears repeating.

Shortcuts by students may easily slip into unethical behavior. The successful case teacher manages to convey to his or her students the worth of self-discovery, of proper preparation and participation, and the pride of accomplishment, so that shortcuts are not particularly appealing.

When one ponders the list of obstacles to effective case teaching in a non-case environment, it is easy to become discouraged and say, "Why should I bother?" There are some good reasons for not giving up so easily, however. The educator who is convinced that the use of cases makes sense for the educational purposes intended and who then is willing to settle for less is not living up to his or her calling. A well taught case session can generate a degree of participant satisfaction and immediate positive feedback that is very rewarding.

Case teaching skills are part of the instructor's capability to teach and work in a participative way. Therefore, they contribute to non-case activities such as class discussions of readings, videos, presentations, team leadership and coaching and, yes, even committee work and chairing meetings. Having teaching experience with the decision making process also has obvious professional and personal life pay-offs.

conclusion

Every teacher using the case method has consciously or subconsciously made at least three major educational decisions. For course content, the major choice was between theory only, application only, or a combination of theory and application. For student involvement in the learning process, the main choice was non-participative versus participative. For materials, the main choice was between non-field or field-based materials.

A desire to cover theory and application in a participative mode with field-based materials called cases results in the case method.

Technological advances have made it possible for students to access high quality content-based education almost anywhere in the world at anytime. What justification can a teacher give to require a student to come to a specific classroom at a specific time? The answer has to be that the learning experience from a face-to-face interchange is so superior to other options that the high cost is justified. Therefore, there is added pressure on the case teacher to assure that every class session is of the highest quality possible. Thus, once the decision to use cases has been reached, the challenge becomes one of effectiveness, the main topic throughout this text.

Since two of the three authors of this book have an operations management background, it is appropriate that the remainder of this chapter takes an operations perspective on the challenges of teaching with cases effectively.

AN OPERATIONS PERSPECTIVE

Our operations perspective has three main parts. The first part deals with the objectives of the system. Here, the relationship between course objectives and case use frequency is identified along with potential implications. The second part is a detailed look at the system components and their interaction. The case learning/teaching process is viewed as an input-transformation-output system and examined accordingly. The third part focuses on the environment within which the system takes place and also raises some technology related issues.

Objectives and Case Use Frequency

An operations viewpoint begins with the examination of an operating system and its objectives. The key managerial question is, "How can the operations manager contribute effectively to organizational objectives and strategies?"

In the context of teaching with cases the parallel question is, "How can the teacher using cases contribute effectively to institutional objectives and strategies?"

As is true in many non-educational institutions, the assumption that organizational objectives and strategies are clearly enumerated and communicated and understood by all "managers" is not realistic. Often, in the absence of strong institutional guidance, the individual instructor is called upon to provide his or her own perception of what the institution is trying to achieve. Attribution of institutional aims is probably seldom accomplished without some personal preference coloration creeping in. Since our interest is in the use of cases, a clear indication of personal preference seems to be the frequency of case use by the instructor.

In our opinion the variation in case use frequency stems largely from a fundamental difference in the educational objectives held by each instructor.

Case use frequency can be expressed as the percentage of total class or course time devoted to cases. It can vary from very low to very high with a full range in between. An attempt has been made in Exhibit 10-1 to examine how the objectives, the role of cases, underlying assumptions, and implications might be different with varying amounts of case use. It is probably best to focus at the low and high use extremes for this purpose, without being explicit about case use frequency.

That cases can be used at either end of the frequency scale attests to their potential flexibility. Whether the same cases should be used on both ends or not may be a matter of dispute.

The middle area between the two extremes is the tough one. Is it possible to achieve the best of both worlds? The lack of data on results makes this a particularly difficult education design challenge. How many cases should an educator use to achieve a minimum level of competence in analytical skills, problem solving, decision making, or communication? How many cases does it take before a student is considered adequate in the application of a particular technique to real life problems? Certain institutions have been able to establish a reputation which solves this problem neatly for the outside world. The institution's "brand name" on the diploma or degree guarantees that the participant has successfully completed the program of instruction and that the "consumers of the product" are willing to buy without worrying about detailed specifications because they have found previous "products" to their liking.

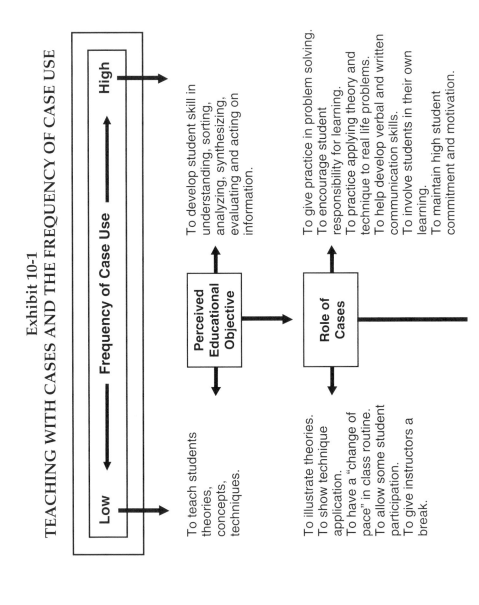

Exhibit 10-1
TEACHING WITH CASES AND THE FREQUENCY OF CASE USE

Frequency of Case Use

Low   High

Perceived Educational Objective

To teach students theories, concepts, techniques.

To develop student skill in understanding, sorting, analyzing, synthesizing, evaluating and acting on information.

Role of Cases

To illustrate theories.
To show technique application.
To have a "change of pace" in class routine.
To allow some student participation.
To give instructors a break.

To give practice in problem solving.
To encourage student responsibility for learning.
To practice applying theory and technique to real life problems.
To help develop verbal and written communication skills.
To involve students in their own learning.
To maintain high student commitment and motivation.

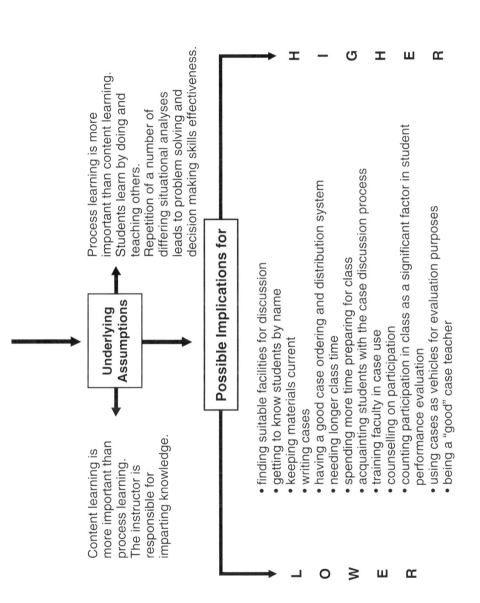

Content learning is more important than process learning. The instructor is responsible for imparting knowledge.

Underlying Assumptions

Process learning is more important than content learning. Students learn by doing and teaching others. Repetition of a number of differing situational analyses leads to problem solving and decision making skills effectiveness.

Possible Implications for

L O W E R

H I G H E R

- finding suitable facilities for discussion
- getting to know students by name
- keeping materials current
- writing cases
- having a good case ordering and distribution system
- needing longer class time
- spending more time preparing for class
- acquainting students with the case discussion process
- training faculty in case use
- counselling on participation
- counting participation in class as a significant factor in student performance evaluation
- using cases as vehicles for evaluation purposes
- being a "good" case teacher

Since, to the operations manager, the final output is a specific result designed into the total process, the process itself, its components, and their interrelationships need to be examined more closely.

The Case Teaching Process as an Input-Transformation-Output System

Teaching with cases can be diagrammed as a simple input-transformation-output system. (See Exhibit 10-2.) This representation can be applied to a single class, as well as to a course, a program, or an institution. Since the interest of most readers is likely to focus on the individual class and the course, discussion will be primarily at these two levels, with only an occasional reference to the program or the institutional focus.

Exhibit 10-2
THE CASE TEACHING PROCESS AS AN
INPUT-TRANSFORMATION-OUTPUT SYSTEM

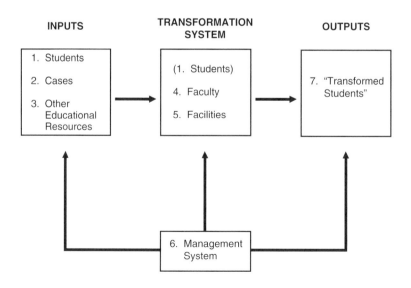

A first glance at what actually constitutes the input-transformation-output system and what is happening as people teach with cases is enough to give it the appearance of a horror show for the serious operations manager. Here is a system without easily measurable output, variable inputs, high variability in the transformation process, ill-defined capacity, and a management system in which responsibilities and authority are diffused. About the only component which can be specified in reasonable form and with acceptable justification is the facility.

A more detailed look at each of the seven components may reveal issues and concerns perhaps not immediately obvious.

1. Students. Students are supposed to be the transformable entities. As distinct from a factory input, one vital role the student learning with cases is supposed to play is to assist in the transformation process. The product transforms itself. It is impossible to achieve a homogeneous student input. Therefore, there is a question of desirable attributes, or prerequisites, not only as to formal education, but also as to personal characteristics, like cultural background, values, leadership, independence, social and communication skills, work experience, entrepreneurial spirit, gender, age, and health.

One of the accusations faced by the "best case schools" is that they only admit the "best students" and, therefore, their output is likely to be good. It is not clear what constitutes the "best" mix of students as input or what attributes are best for the use of teaching/learning with cases. Nor is it clear what is a desirable minimum or maximum number of students that can be put into a course in which cases will be used. General practice seems to limit total class size to a maximum of about one hundred students. What the trade-off in educational quality would be between two classes of 50 students each, versus one of 100, both taught with the same instructor and identical course outline, is not clear.

The suitable age of students to consider the use of cases lies between 12 and 100 years. Some experiments have been tried with even younger groups. What mix of ages in a course is desirable is not clear, although in management programs, a 30 year differential between youngest and oldest class members is not unusual.

Motivation of the student to learn is probably the single most dominant factor in education. In the case method students can be more motivated, since they can appreciate the relevance of what they are doing and become actively involved in the process. Instructors can do many things to add to this motivation as is evident throughout this book. Some relatively simple but basic actions include getting to know one's students well; grading case exams personally and handing them back quickly; showing concern in and out of class for student progress and problems with participation.

2. Cases. Cases are the differentiating characteristic between case teaching and other forms of instruction. A case is a description of an actual situation, commonly involving a challenge, opportunity, decision or problem faced by a person in an organization. A case is field-based and contains primary source data. A case is a selected story; not the case writer's story but the decision maker's story. Moreover, someone in the organization has released the case to the case writer's organization thereby giving official permission to use the case for educational purposes.

How long a case should be, how it should be organized, how much information should be provided of the relevant and non-relevant kind, how old or new, what kind of managerial position in what type of organization, and where in the world, are only some of the questions the instructor faces in the course design task. Despite the existence of ECCH and other case distribution centers, access to cases still faces hurdles. There is a huge challenge in developing a continuous flow of new cases, truly reflecting the reality of the changing managerial tasks and new environments. And how does one tell whether a case is any good at all? Best sellers lists identify those used more frequently. Are these necessarily the best? Various attempts to set up a case refereeing process exist in different parts of the world. What the consequences of these actions will be is not entirely clear. Will it encourage more academics to turn to case development? Will it produce more good cases? Will it create two classes of cases: refereed or good ones and others? Will it raise the overall quality level of cases?

How many cases it takes to accomplish a specific educational objective is a question already raised above. Some research has at least begun to compare cases to games, simulations, and exercises on the assumption that relatively few cases would be used. Obviously, an individual case can address a multiplicity of objectives simultaneously. Our Case Difficulty Cube, with the analytical, conceptual and presentation dimensions, provides a way of organizing key learning objectives with cases. The multiplicity of objectives makes the case selection task difficult for the instructor. A case is not just simply a good linear programming application, or a good break-even analysis example. It has other dimensions that may make it more or less desirable for the course under consideration.

The assumption that the right case will necessarily be fully appreciated by students is naive. So many factors impinge on the transformation process, that the case itself may not be dominant. It is possible for an instructor to have a good class with a "bad" case, and a bad class with a "good" case. The tenacity with which some instructors cling to their favorite cases may be partially explained by a belief that the case itself is the dominant factor. The case needs to be seen in context, not only in terms of topic or theoretical coverage, but also in its other dimensions. Envisaging a process whereby the case may be taught is a skill not born into every teacher. The trend towards greater concentration on and sharing of teaching notes, as integral with the case writing and distribution process, is a healthy recognition of this fact.

It is our belief that the participatory aspect of case teaching gives the case its greatest powers. Thus, the case needs to be sufficiently interesting for a student to prepare it properly. The assurance and expectation that the student's insights and analyses will be seriously considered and appreciated in class will be the valuable motivators for the student to do the necessary preparation.

3. Other Educational Inputs. On a course basis, other educational inputs will vary in quantity inversely with the frequency of case use. What constitutes a proper mix of lectures, simulations, exercises, readings, discussions, videos, computerized learning programs, problems, with cases and how each interacts with the other is something each instructor must face in course design, despite a scarcity of supporting data. Interestingly enough, "what the instructor is good at" is itself an important consideration. A good case teacher is probably wise to use cases more than an instructor less comfortable with this method.

Even in the early days of using cases for management education, the dichotomy between imparting knowledge and developing people to make decisions and take action was clearly recognized. With the knowledge explosion and the increasing pressure for academic respectability, this dichotomy appears to grow larger. Fortunately, the computer has made available new options, such as electronic cases, interactive learning, business games, and a variety of exercises which help bridge the gap. There have been, therefore, strong pressures for "case method" schools to give up class time formerly reserved for cases to other educational inputs. This process has already gone on for a considerable time and has resulted in a significant decrease in time spent on cases. The increasing number of options available to every teacher makes proper choice more difficult. The accompanying blurring of objectives and boundaries between inputs means the choice is no longer simply lecture or use a case.

4. *Faculty.* The instructor is not just a worker on the educational assembly line. Normally, he or she has a significant managerial and leadership role at the same time. On an individual course basis, the instructor may be seen as an individual craftsperson. In the use of cases, a student role may also be expected of the instructor. The teacher becomes transformed along with the student. What kind of person is best suited to the case discussion leader's role has been amply speculated on.

What constitutes an acceptable instructor load in terms of case teaching and how much time should be allocated for preparation for a case class, the teaching of the class, and additional student contact? Institutional norms on this question have been developed, but variations between institutions are substantial. How does an instructor get evaluated on a results basis? Is student reaction the proper way to go? Research has shown that, for non-case courses, teacher popularity and student learning do not always correlate positively. Does the same hold for case courses?

What turns the instructor "on" when using cases? Is it the excitement of participants, fun of dealing with the real life problem, the hunt for truth, self-fulfillment? Certainly, in many institutions the reward-punishment system does not favor case teaching, or anything else associated with cases. The low esteem given to the use of cases may have been partially fostered by past incompetent instructors. Nevertheless, for the younger instructor in particular, it may represent a horrendous hurdle in the immediate peer environment. Ways need to be found to increase the legitimacy of teaching with cases on bases other than faith alone.

5. Facilities. Facilities can do so much to support the effective use of cases or so much to block results, that they are a significant component in the process. Since facilities well suited to case teaching can easily be used for other methodologies, including lectures, the argument for building in the case option is extremely strong. The argument gains even more validity when one recognizes the institutional obstacles to facility change, once in place. Even though the classroom is the key unit under consideration, support facilities such as small group discussion areas easily accessible to students, reproduction and distribution facilities for cases, and easy library and Internet access can lend valuable support.

6. Management System. The management system provides the design, operation and control of the transformation process. It gives commands and receives feedback. In the teaching with cases context, the responsibilities and authority within the managerial system are diffused. The instructor bears certain ones individually: identification of course objectives, case selection in course design, execution of the Case Teaching Plan on a regular basis and responsibility for measuring student performance are typical examples. Responsibility for facilities usually lies somewhere outside the academic stream in teaching institutions. Student admission may be handled by a registrar's office and case ordering, reproduction and distribution by two or three separate bodies. Timetabling may fall anywhere and supervision of faculty takes a variety of interesting forms. The point need not be belabored; considerable coordination is required to make sure that the whole makes sense.

The management system is also supposed to provide suitable motivation for the student to learn and the instructor to teach (both to the best of their respective capabilities), take measures of actual results and initiate corrective action. To a large extent these aspects are often left to the individual teacher.

When a process analysis is carried out, two major concerns from an operations viewpoint deal with capacity and bottlenecks. Ideally, a system should be run close to capacity and be well balanced, with few, if any, bottlenecks. As has already been mentioned, capacity in case teaching is a flexible concept. The number of students in a class, the number of cases teachable in a working day, the number of case preparations or classes by students per day are all basic measures necessary to arrive at some form of capacity consensus. Combining such simple quantity considerations with quality or functional objectives increases the measurement problem. "How many students out of the total class learned well from this experience?" is more relevant than, "How many students were present?"

The concept of a bottleneck is related to a capacity constraint, limiting the systems output. Potential bottlenecks may be: (1) the students – some or all not prepared properly, or without the necessary skills to handle the case; (2) the facilities – blocking effective learning; (3) the faculty – unskilled or lacking in motivation; or (4) the management system – poorly designed and/or operated. The lack of congruence among system components creates an out-of-balance and out-of-focus condition.

7. The Output: The "Transformed" Students. Normally, if a system output meets quality, cost, quantity and delivery requirements, the system is a long way on the right track. The assumption is made that the process which produced the output must be, generally, in acceptable order. Measuring the output of a case class, or a course using a significant number of cases, is no easy task. Therefore, the management job of relating output to system component performance is difficult to execute. At what point should a case be substituted, a Case Teaching Plan modified, a class lengthened or shortened? These are some relatively simple questions, but illustrative of the point.

One way to respond is to let the market forces have free play, "As long as our students are being hired, we must be doing alright." That may give too strong a credit to market sensitivity. Moreover, much of the discussion to this point has assumed that the purpose of the educational process has been to respond to foreseeable market requirements.

What will our current students be required to do twenty or thirty years from now? What skills will they be required to have? What role will additional training on and off the job have to play? What should our contribution be now so that the base for that future career will be appropriate? Is it even realistic to think in today's educational world that current education might still have an impact two or three decades later? Or should we just be teaching our students to be able to learn from their future experiences?

The Environment

The academic environment for degree programs in management is currently unsettled in many institutions. High student demand coupled with tightening purse strings, and tougher promotion and tenure rules put pressures on the academic to get the product out without much institutional support in the form of additional resources. Since it is probably easier to process large numbers of students using non-case courses, changing the status quo from non or low case use to higher case use is undoubtedly difficult. In fact, pressures will favor conversion in the other direction.

The Technology

The technology in education is changing and must, of necessity, have an impact on the process chosen for the transformation system. Do the computer and the Internet spell a fundamentally new approach to case teaching? Is an electronic or video case still a case? Have the processes of production and the requirements of the medium altered the original data to such an extent that a similarity exists, but no more? If actors are used to portray the roles of people in the same situation, does this make it a play? When all of the financial statements of an organization are stored in a computer and students are asked to analyze them, does this constitute a case or an exercise?

Various institutions are currently attempting to use cases via the Internet. What happens to the standard Three Stage Learning Process? Do notice boards or chat rooms constitute effective small group discussion? Are multiple choice case questions a substitute for class discussion? Is there a completely different approach to the use of cases?

CONCLUSION

It is certainly easier to identify challenges and problems in teaching with cases than to solve them. And it is to be expected that the future will bring new opportunities and new challenges. Teaching with cases is not stagnant. The case method is advancing and the directions in which it appears to be going have exciting promises. There is no one best way to teach with cases. Not only do objectives for using cases vary, but so do students, instructors, facilities, and environments. This variability complicates the process. However, it gives the individual instructor an opportunity to custom build an approach suitable to his or her unique situation.

Over the years we have experimented with a variety of tools, concepts and techniques that might help simplify and increase the effectiveness of case writing, learning and teaching. Of these, the prime teaching/learning tools are the Case Difficulty Cube, the Three Stage Learning Process, the Case Preparation Chart and the Case Teaching Plan. We are convinced that this text can make a significant difference for those instructors interested in improving their case teaching performance.

Our concern has always been with improving the effectiveness of case writing, learning and teaching while minimizing the time required. The teaching task is intensely personal yet highly public. The effective case teacher earns not only an immediate positive response from his or her students but also their lifelong appreciation for a job well done.

Appendix 1
DIMENSIONAL LAYOUTS OF CLASSROOMS
DESIGNED FOR CASE DISCUSSION

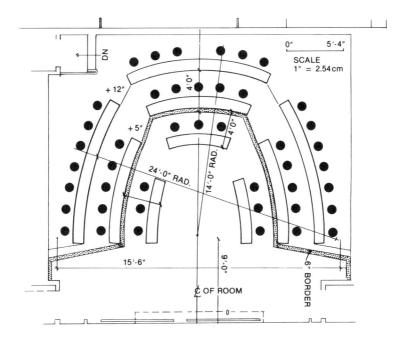

a) A 44 seat classroom layout*

---
* Courtesy Ron Murphy, architect, London, Ontario

Appendix 1 (continued)

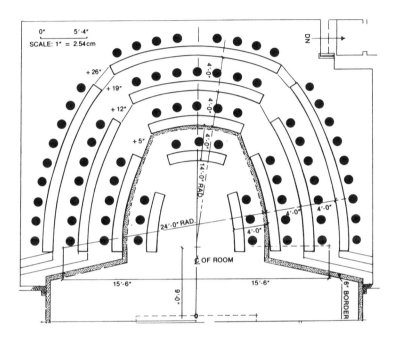

a) A 71 seat classroom layout*

* Courtesy Ron Murphy, architect, London, Ontario

Appendix 2

MAJOR CASE DISTRIBUTION
CENTRES OF THE WORLD

The European Case Clearing House (ECCH)
at Cranfield University   Tel: +44 (0)1234 750903
Wharley End, Bedfordshire   Fax: +44 (0)1234 751125
MK43 0JR UK
E-mail: **ECCH@cranfield.ac.uk**
Web site: **www.ecch.cranfield.ac.uk/**

at Babson College   Tel: +1 781 239 5884
Babson Park,   Fax: +1 781 239 5885
Wellesly, MA 02457 USA
E-mail: **ECCH@babson@aol.com**
Web site: **www.ecchatbabson.org**

ECCH distributes cases from the following major case
producing management schools of the world:

Darden Business School at University of Virginia*
Harvard Business School*
John F. Kennedy School of
    Government at Harvard University*
IESE, Barcelona
IMD, Lausanne
INSEAD, Fontainebleau
London Business School
Richard Ivey School of Business at
    The University of Western Ontario*
School of Management at Cranfield University
Stanford University*

* ECCH does not distribute this material in the United States
  or Canada

Appendix 2 (continued)

Harvard Business School
Harvard Business School Publishing
Customer Service Department   Tel: +1 800 545 7685
60 Harvard Way   + 1 617 783 7600
Boston, MA 02163, USA   Fax: +1 617 783 7666
E-mail: **custserv@hbsp.harvard.edu**
Web site: **www.hbsp.harvard.edu/**

(Harvard Business School Publishing also distributes Ivey cases in the US.)

Richard Ivey School of Business
Ivey Publishing   Tel: +1 519 661 3208
Richard Ivey School of Business   +1 800 649 6355
The University of Western Ontario   Fax: +1 519 661 3882
London, Ontario,
Canada, N6A 3K7
E-mail: **cases@ivey.uwo.ca**
Web site: **www.ivey.uwo.ca/cases**

(Ivey also distributes Harvard cases and Harvard Business Review reprints in Canada.)

Darden Business School
The Darden Case Collection   Tel: +1 800 246 3367
Darden Business School   Fax: +1 434 924 4859
University of Virginia
P.O. Box 6550
Charlottesville, VA   22906-6550, USA
E-mail: **dardencases@virginia.edu**
Web site: **www.darden.virginia.edu/**

Appendix 3

Richard Ivey School of Business
The University of Western Ontario

IVEY

CASE WRITING WORKSHOP

NIXON TRAILERS INC.

Bill Cook, materials manager at Nixon Trailers Inc. in Lancaster, Pennsylvania, was considering a proposal from his purchasing agent to outsource manufacturing for an outrigger bracket. It was the end of April, 2000, and Bill Cook had to evaluate the proposal and decide whether to proceed.

NIXON TRAILERS INC. BACKGROUND

Nixon Trailers Inc. (Nixon) manufactured trailers for highway transport trucks. The company comprised three divisions, the Trailer, Sandblast & Paint, and Metal Fabricating Divisions. Each division operated as a separate profit center, but manufacturing operations between each were highly integrated. The Metal Fabricating Division produced most of the component parts of the trailers, the Trailer Division performed the assembly operations, and the Sandblast & Paint Division was responsible for the sandblasting and final painting operation. Nixon manufactured approximately 40 trailers per year, with about two-thirds of their annual products produced during the period from November to April.

THE OUTRIGGER BRACKET

The outrigger bracket, part number T-178, was an accessory that could be used to secure oversized containers. The bracket consisted of four component parts welded together, and each trailer sold by Nixon had 20 brackets, ten per side.

The Metal Fabricating Division was presently manufacturing the outrigger bracket. The subassembly parts, T-67, T-75, T-69 and T-77, were processed on a burn table machine, which cut the raw material to

Yasheng Chen prepared this case solely to provide material for class discussion during the 2000 Case Writing Workshop held at the Richard Ivey School of Business under the supervision of Professors James A. Erskine and Michiel R. Leenders. The author does not intend to illustrate either effective or ineffective handling of a managerial situation. The author may have disguised certain names and other identifying information to protect confidentiality.

Appendix 3 (continued)

size. Although the burn table machine could work with 8 burn stations, this machine only had only been operating with one station. The final assembly operation, T-70, was performed at a manual welding station.

Manufacturing lead-time for the outrigger bracket was two weeks. However, the Fabrication Division had been able to coordinate supply and production with assembly operations. Consequently, finished inventory levels of the outrigger bracket were kept to a minimum. Nixon estimated its inventory holding costs were 20 percent per annum.

THE OUTSOURCING DECISION

In an effort to reduce costs, the purchasing agent, Wendy Sinclair, who reported to Bill Cook, solicited quotes from three local companies to supply the outrigger bracket. Mayes Steel Fabricators (Mayes), a current supplier to Nixon for other components, offered the lowest bid, with a cost of $108.20, FOB Nixon.

Bill met with the controller, Nick Simpson, who provided a breakdown of the manufacturing costs for the outrigger bracket. Looking at the spreadsheet, Nick commented: "These are based on estimates of our costs from this year's budget. Looking at the material, labor and overhead costs, I would estimate that the fixed costs for this part are in the area of about 20 percent. Keep in mind that it costs us about $75 to place an order with our vendors." Exhibit 1 provides Nixon's internal cost breakdown and details from the quote from Mayes.

Bill expected that Nixon would have to arrange for extra storage space if he decided to outsource the outrigger bracket to Mayes, who had quoted delivery lead-time of four weeks. Since Mayes was local and had a good track record, Bill didn't expect the need to carry much safety stock, but the order quantity issue still needed to be resolved.

Nixon was operating in a very competitive environment and Bill had been asked by the division general manager to look for opportunities to reduce costs. As he sat down to review the information, Bill knew that he should make a decision quickly if it was possible to cut costs by outsourcing the outrigger bracket.

Appendix 3 (continued)

Exhibit 1

NIXON TRAILERS INC.
Manufacturing Costs and Mayes Quote: Outrigger Bracket T-178

Parts	Mayes Steel Fabricators	Nixon Manufacturing Costs
T-67	$14.60	$17.92
T-75	$21.10	$17.92
T-69	$18.50	$45.20
T-77	$13.00	$10.37
T-70	$41.00	$58.69
Total	$108.20	$150.10

Appendix 3 (continued)

Richard Ivey School of Business
The University of Western Ontario

CASE WRITING WORKSHOP

TEACHING NOTE

NIXON TRAILERS INC.

SYNOPSIS

Bill Cook, materials manager at Nixon Trailers Inc. in Lancaster, Pennsylvania, was considering a proposal from his purchasing agent to outsource manufacturing for an outrigger bracket. It was the end of April, 2000, and Bill Cook had to evaluate the proposal and decide whether to proceed.

TEACHING OBJECTIVES

This case was written for practitioners in the supply area as well as undergraduate students in a supply course. The case requires students to simultaneously evaluate the issues of outsourcing and inventory lot sizing. It can also be used to cover EOQ applications and supplier cost analysis.

IMMEDIATE ISSUES

Should Nixon outsource the outrigger bracket to Mayes Steel Fabricators?

If the outrigger bracket was outsourced, how should concerns for lead times and order quantities be addressed?

BASIC ISSUES

1. Outsourcing
2. Lot sizing
3. Economic order quantity theory
4. Cost analysis
5. The role of purchasing in continuous improvement

P. Fraser Johnson prepared this teaching note solely to provide material for class discussion during the 2000 Case Writing Workshop held at the Richard Ivey School of Business under the supervision of Professors James A. Erskine and Michiel R. Leenders. The author does not intend to illustrate either effective or ineffective handling of a managerial situation. The author may have disguised certain names and other identifying information to protect confidentiality.

                                   Version: 00-08-25

Appendix 3 (continued)

SUGGESTED STUDENT ASSIGNMENT

If you were in the position of Bill Cook:
1. What would be your analysis of the opportunity to outsource the outrigger bracket? What would you do and why?
2. If Nixon was to outsource the outrigger bracket to Mayes, what lot sizes would you specify and why? (Note: You must address this question, regardless of your response to Question 1.)

POTENTIAL DISCUSSION QUESTIONS FOR USE IN CLASS

1. Do you think Nixon should outsource the bracket? Why or why not?
2. What do you think of the quote from Mayes? How would you respond? What information would you request?
3. What would you say to the plant manager?
4. Are the cost savings sufficient enough to move the business to Mayes?
5. Is it appropriate to use the EOQ formula here to establish the lot size? Do all of the EOQ assumptions hold here?

CASE ANALYSIS

This case requires some quantitative analysis if the students are going to develop a meaningful analysis. First, let's take a look at the cost data for the outrigger bracket. The case indicates that Nixon produces 40 trailers per year, which suggests that it needs 800 brackets annually, assuming 20 brackets per trailer. Nixon estimated its bracket costs at $150.10 each, for a total annual cost of $120,080. It is certainly worthwhile for Bill Cook and Wendy Sinclair to spend some time on this project.

Exhibit 1 in the case provides the data from the controller, Nick Simpson, and the detail from the quote from Mayes. Note the inconsistencies between the prices from Mayes and Nixon's costs. This raises the issue of the accuracy of the prices/costs. It suggests that either Nixon doesn't have a good handle on its costs or Mayes has made some mistakes in its bid. It would be worthwhile to follow-up on this issue with the controller, Nick Simpson, and with Mayes. Students should be prepared to show how they intend to reconcile the inconsistencies. It would be useful to get more information, such as material and direct labor costs. Likely the material costs represent the bulk of the costs for the four subassembly parts.

Appendix 3 (continued)

Exhibit TN 1 provides an analysis of the costs from the exhibit in the case, incorporating the fixed and variable components of Nixon's costs. This analysis indicates a difference of $11.89 per part, or potential savings of $9,512 per year or 8 percent of the total current cost if the bracket is 100 percent outsourced. (Note that fixed costs should be removed from comparison figures).

Part T-69 is an interesting example. Maybe most of the benefit of outsourcing can be obtained by having Mayes produce T-69. This is the gray zone in make or buy referred to by the course text. Sometimes the better solution lies between 100 percent make and 100 percent buy. If $17.66 in variable cost can be saved on T-69 then this would represent 800 x $17.66 = $14,128 in savings.

Lot Sizing and Inventory

The case infers that Nixon's manufacturing and assembly operations do a pretty good job synchronizing their inventories and Nixon carries very little finished inventory as a result. However, the case also suggests that Bill Cook had to establish a lot size quantity in the event that Mayes was chosen as the source for the bracket. In any event, it would appear that finished component inventories for the outrigger bracket would be increasing.

There is sufficient information in the case for the students to calculate the EOQ. The following is provided in the case:

D = 800 units per year
i = 20 percent
C = $108.2
S = $75   Please note this $75 is highly suspicious. Is this all variable
    cost?

$$EOQ = \sqrt{\frac{2DS}{iC}}$$

$$EOQ = \sqrt{\frac{2\,(800)\,(75)}{.20\,(108.2)}}$$

$$EOQ = 74.5 \text{ brackets}$$

Appendix 3 (continued)

Before going any further, it must be made clear this situation breaks at least one of the underlying assumptions of the EOQ formula, constant demand. However, the EOQ formula is fairly robust and should provide a reasonable estimate of the appropriate order quantity.

The EOQ calculation suggests an order quantity of 75 brackets. Bill might want to adjust this slightly to match the 80 units needed for four trailers. Assuming an average inventory of 40 units, the carrying costs would be $865.60 (40 _ $108.20 _ 0.20) and the order costs would be $750 (10 orders at $75), for a total cost of $1,615.60, not enough to reverse the verdict.

For T-69 alone the EOQ would be $EOQ = \sqrt{\dfrac{2(800)(75)}{.20(18.50)}} = 180$

Other Considerations

There is a solid opportunity here for Bill Cook, assuming that the numbers from Nick Simpson and Mayes are accurate. However, this does not mean that Nixon should outsource the bracket, at least right away. After checking the numbers with Nick and Mayes, Bill might want to dig into process improvement opportunities before committing to outsourcing. For example, the case indicates that Nixon is not getting full benefit from the eight station burn table machine. The threat of moving production out to a supplier might create some interest in the plant to changing the process to reduce costs. Either way, Bill might want to satisfy manufacturing that he gave them a fair chance to look at the process and its costs before pulling the business.

TEACHING SUGGESTIONS

The case discussion can start with the motivation for outsourcing. Touch on the annual costs of the bracket and what might be a reasonable cost savings to justify moving production to Mayes. For example, would you move it for a savings of 1 percent? How about 10 percent?

Next, look at the costs and prices in the exhibit in the case. Press the students on the inconsistencies and what they might do about it. A statement like this might be appropriate: "Just because someone gives you a number, should you trust it?"

Appendix 3 (continued)

Next, move into the cost analysis. Get out the fixed and variable components of Nixon's costs and ask the students how they could use the data. Following this discussion, ask about lot sizing. The students should understand at this point that there are potential savings, so they should give some thought to how much should be ordered per batch. Someone should bring up the EOQ formula (especially if a reading about EOQs has been assigned), if not you might have to raise using this technique.

Near the end of class you can start to ask for what the students want to do and how they would implement their plan. Make them consider how they want to handle the matter with the manufacturing group at Nixon and what information they may want from Mayes.

Exhibit TN 1

OUTRIGGER BRACKET COST ANALYSIS

Part	Nixon Fixed Costs (20 % Total Cost)	Nixon Variable Costs (80 % Total Cost)	Mayes Quote	Difference Nixon Variable and Mayes Quote
T-67	$ 3.58	$ 14.34	$ 14.60	($ 0.26)
T-75	$ 3.58	$ 14.34	$ 21.10	($ 6.76)
T-69	$ 9.04	$ 36.16	$ 18.50	$ 17.66
T-77	$ 2.07	$ 8.30	$ 13.00	($ 4.70)
T-70	$ 11.74	$ 46.95	$ 41.00	$ 5.95
Total	$ 30.01	$ 120.09	$ 108.20	$ 11.89

Appendix 3 (continued)

CASE PREPARATION CHART

Case Title: Nixon Trailers Inc.

Case Assignment: If you were in the position of Bill Cook: (1) Analysis of proposal – accept? (2) Lot size?

I. SHORT CYCLE PROCESS

Name　　　　Position

Who: Bill Cook, Materials Manager

Issue(s)

What: Outsource outrigger brackets? Lot size? Accept P.A. proposal?

Why: Save money

When: ASAP

Case Difficulty Cube

How: (___2___ , ___2-3___ , ___1___)
Analytical, Conceptual, Presentation

II. LONG CYCLE PROCESS

A. Issue(s)

Immediate

1. Approve proposal
2. Lot size
3.

Basic

1. Make or buy
2. Outsourcing
3. Cost analysis
4. Lot sizing

B. Case Data Analysis
See attached teaching note

II. LONG CYCLE PROCESS (continued)

C. Alternative Generation

1. Outsource 100%
2. Outsource partial – T - 69
3. Keep in house
4. Improve OPS & keep in House
5. 4+2

D. Decision Criteria

1. Cost
2. Quality
3. Availability
4. Bottom line impact

E. Alternative Assessment　#5

Quantitative	⊕		N		–			
Qualitative	⊕	N	–	+	N	–	+	N	–
Decision	go	go	?	?	no	no	?	no	no

F. Preferred Alternative – Depends on whether process improvements possible in house

Predicted Outcome – Minimum savings target $14,000

G. Action & Implementation Plan

Timing
Milestones

Who　　Bill Cook
What　Talk to PA/Prod'n
When　ASAP
Where
How　　Process imp'ts possible, partial outsource? T-69

Missing Information – Why discrepancies between supplier quote and internal costs

Assumptions – By going outside savings in labor and material would actually be Mayes. Makes most likely source.

Reference: *Learning with Cases*, 2001, page 36

Appendix 3 (continued)

CASE TEACHING PLAN

Case _Nixon Trailers Inc._   **Course** _SCM 101_   **Date** _March 5, 2003_

Time Plan   **Agenda**   **Participation Plan**

____ 1. Introduction

Volunteer Preferences	
1. Janet Ho	5. Art Sheppard
2. Bill Sanders	6. Ron Smit
3. Lena Ashton	7. Annette Valois
4. Bob Quinn	8. Jorge Torres

        Agenda for class

____ 2. Next/Other Classes – March 10
        Johnson Controls case
        Chapter 9 – Price – P&SM

____ 3. Comments, Questions   **Volunteer (V)**   **Call List**

____ 4. Reading Discussion Ch 8 - Outsourcing   V or _Vasily Bronski, Edna Towne_
        pp, 300-308 P&SM

____ 5. Case Introduction   V or _____

____ 6. Teaching Aids

       7. Assignment Questions

        If you were in the position of: Bill Cook

40-45   1 _Analysis, outsource? Why?_   V or _Chris Adamson, Joan Breton, Alex Szabo_

20-25   2 _If outsource, then lot size?_   (V) or _____

____   3 _____   V or _____

____   4 _____   V or _____

_5_ 8. Conclusion   1. Make or buy vs. outsourcing, insourcing
                     2. Fixed vs. variable costs
_80_ Total   3. Supply role

Board Plan

Analysis – Q.1	Decision Criteria	Question 2
	Alternatives	
	Action	

Reference: _Teaching with Cases_, 2003, page 82

index

refereed, 231
role of. See Case method,
  reasons for using
sample, 244-46
sources of, 37, 38, 242-43
timing, 59, 60. See also Case,
  obsolescence
use variations. See Variations,
  case use
with different cultural
  background. See Diversity
video, 200, 237
Case Difficulty Cube, 3, 41-44, 46, 47
  51, 59, 61-62, 66, 117, 180, 231
analytical dimension , 42-43, 75
conceptual dimension , 44, 75
presentation dimension, 42, 43,
  44, 75, 200
Case discussion, 104-12
action/implementation plan, 111-12
alternatives and decision, 108-10
conclusion, 85-86, 113-15
decision criteria, 105, 108, 110.
  See also Decision criteria
issue and analysis, 106-08
problem identification, 72, 106-07
start, 83-85, 101-06. See also
  Beginning of class, preparation of
Case material problems, 137-42,
  161, 231-32. See also Case,
  evaluation
assumptions, 139-40
missing information, 49, 60,
  137-39, 161, 213
quality issues, 141-42, 231
questions in class, 140-41
Case method. See also Participatory
  education; Teaching with cases
context, 11-12
definition, 9-12
familiarization workshops, 211-12
  See also Workshops, case
  teaching
growth, 8

how to introduce, 65-66
number of cases required, 10, 12
  See also Case use frequency
reasons for using, 8, 19, 50,
  226-27, 234
schools, 11, 24, 36, 229, 233
terminology clarification, 9-12
Case on Line Information System.
  See COLIS
Case Preparation Chart, 2, 5, 45,
  46-50, 51, 58, 66, 80, 81, 90, 115,
  117, 178, 182, 195, 252
Case selection. See Course planning;
  Evaluation, of materials; Material
  logistics; Sources of cases
Case teaching
in current academic
  environment, 237
new technology, 237
Case Teaching Plan, 2, 6, 74, 81, 82,
  88, 89-90, 129, 143, 164-65, 234,
  253. See also Evaluation, Case
  Teaching Plan
agenda, 82, 83-86
board plan, 82, 89-90, 159-60
participation plan, 82, 87-89, 159
time plan, 82, 86-87, 158-59. See
  also Time management
Case teaching process as
  input-output system, 228-237
1. students as input, 229-30
2. cases as input, 230-32
3. other educational inputs, 232-33.
  See also Course planning,
  material selection
4. faculty, 233-34
5. facilities, 234. See also Physical
  facilities; Non-case
  environment, case use in
6. management system, 234-36
7. students as output, 236. See
  also Evaluation, participant
Case teaching workshops. See
  Training, teacher